Mass Murder in the United States

Ronald M. Holmes, Ed.D.

University of Louisville

Stephen T. Holmes, Ph.D.

University of Central Florida

Prentice Hall

Upper Saddle River, New Jersey 07458

Library of Congress Cataloging-in-Publication Data

Holmes, Ronald M.
   Mass murder in the United States / Ronald M. Holmes, Stephen T. Holmes.
      p. cm.
   Includes bibliographical references and index.
   ISBN 0-13-934308-3
    1. Mass murder--United States. 2. Criminal psychology--United States. 3.
   Criminals--Identification--United States. 4. Mass murder investigation--United States. I.
   Holmes, Stephen. II. Title.

HV6529 .M64 2000
364.15'23'0973--dc21   00-055055

Senior Acquisitions Editor: Kim Davies
Associate Editor: Marion Gottlieb
Production Editor: Naomi Sysak
Production Liaison: Adele M. Kupchik
Director of Manufacturing and Production: Bruce Johnson
Managing Editor: Mary Carnis
Manufacturing Buyer: Ed O'Dougherty
Art Director: Marianne Frasco
Senior Design Coordinator: Miguel Ortiz
Marketing Manager: Chris Ruel
Marketing Assistant: Joe Toohey
Editorial Assistant: Lisa Schwartz
Cover Design: Joe Sengotta
Cover Image: Guy Crittenden, SIS/Images.Com
Interior Design and Composition: Naomi Sysak
Printer/Binder: R.R. Donnelley, Harrisonburg, VA
Cover Printer: Phoenix

Prentice-Hall International (UK) Limited, London
Prentice-Hall of Australia Pty. Limited, Sydney
Prentice-Hall Canada Inc., Toronto
Prentice-Hall Hispanoamericana, S.A., Mexico
Prentice-Hall of India Private Limited, New Delhi
Prentice-Hall of Japan, Inc., Tokyo
Prentice-Hall Singapore Pte. Ltd.
Editora Prentice-Hall do Brasil, Ltda., Rio de Janeiro

10 9 8 7 6 5 4 3 2

ISBN: 0-13-934308-3

Contents

CHAPTER 4

The Disciple Mass Killer   39

CHAPTER 5

The Family Annihilator   49

CHAPTER 6

The Disgruntled Employee Mass Killer   63

CHAPTER 7

The Ideological Mass Killer   75

CHAPTER 8

The Set-and-Run Mass Killer   87

CHAPTER 9

The Disgruntled Citizen Mass Killer   95

Dedication

This book is dedicated to the memories of the victims of mass murder and their families.

Nothing can be done to erase the terrible pain. Time may reduce the suffering of survivors, but they, too, are victims of the mass killer. Let us never forget.

Preface and Acknowledgments

The writing of any book is a major undertaking. This is true not only in the world of fiction but also in an academic setting. First, one has to be concerned that the topic of the book will be interesting to the reader as well as worthy of the energy necessary for successful completion of a meaningful book. Steve and I have co-authored several books on murder and other topics: *Profiling Violent Crimes, Serial Murder*, and *Contemporary Perspectives in Serial Murder*. In each of these endeavors we were dedicated to the work and decided that the end product was worth the effort.

Our work in the past has centered around homicide in general and serial murder in particular. We have been able to gather valuable information about serial murder from a variety of sources, including personal interviews with serial killers and with police officers, prosecutors, and defense attorneys involved in serial murder cases. However, as we gathered our research data and information, it became more clear to us that there is another form of multicide that may present a more clear and present danger to our fellow citizens: mass murder.

The mass killer problem deserves special attention for several reasons. First, there is general confusion among many as to exactly what mass murder is. It is one of three forms of multicide in the United States, the other two being serial murder and spree murder. Most Americans are familiar with serial killers. The names of Larry Eyler, Ted Bundy, John Gacy, Henry Lucas, Glenn Rogers, and many others are household names and have become a part of American folklore. Even spree killers such as Bonnie and Clyde or Carol Fugate and Charles Starkweather are well-known names. With the exception of certain mass killers— Charles Whitman, Timothy McVeigh, and perhaps John List—most mass killers are invisible to the American public and receive little media attention. The Federal Bureau of Investigation estimates that there are about 35 serial murderers currently killing in the United States. The exact number is unknown. What we have found is that mass killers may be responsible for more murders each year than the known number of victims of serial killers.

There are other differences between mass and serial killers. For instance, a serial killer often kills complete strangers. On the other hand, the victims of mass killings typically are known to the killer. The common wisdom concerning this phenomenon suggests that the victims are equally likely to be strangers to both types of killers. This is not true, and this was one of the findings that surprised us in the writing of this book. There were others.

For example, the American public cannot protect itself from mass killers. With a serial killer, a general sense of awareness and refusal to place oneself in precarious and vulnerable circumstances reduce the individual risk of victimization. The same thing cannot be said in a mass murder scenario. Although steps can be taken to identify disgruntled employees or citizens or refer them for counseling, there is simply no way to engage self-protective measures to avoid falling prey to mass killers. Citizens cannot simply avoid walking alone at night or refuse to pick up hitchhikers. Unfortunately, with the mass killer, especially one who kills victims outside his or her family, there is often no behavior that can limit their vulnerability to attack. Thus from a broad perspective, each of us is at risk of becoming a victim of this type of crime, regardless of occupation or any lifestyle choice.

This book is deliberately arranged to lead the reader onto a path of understanding the mass murder problem and the various types of mass killers. For example, in Chapter 1, we deal with the basic definitions and statistics of the mass murder problem. We then move into a short examination of the history of the mass murder phenomenon. We deal with an older case of mass murder, the Charles Whitman shooting atop the University of Texas's clock tower, and follow it with the more recent case of Michael Carneal. This teenager went into his high school in western Kentucky and killed three schoolmates and wounded several others.

In the third chapter we develop a typology of mass murder and discuss the theory and classification of mass murder types. The behavioral backgrounds, motivations, anticipated gains, spatial mobility, and victim characteristics are discussed, with an emphasis on how these items affect the classification of mass murder types.

The next series of chapters deal with the various types of mass killers:

- The disciple mass killer
- The family annihilator
- The disgruntled employee mass killer
- The ideological mass killer
- The set-and-run mass killer
- The disgruntled citizen mass killer
- The psychotic mass killer
- School shooters

The final chapter presents some of the community reactions and problems in a mass murder investigation. The problems discussed deal with how cases are labeled and defined as mass murders, turf issues, determination of the type of mass killer, the training and education of law enforcement professionals, and identification of victims.

In each chapter we have introduced cases that illustrate the type of mass killer we are addressing. Looking at a particular case helps us understand the mentality of a mass killer. At the beginning of each chapter we have included short vignettes of mass killers to set the stage for the discussion in that chapter.

The goal of the book is to present to readers a comprehensive and readable treatment of this social issue. By examining each type of mass killer within a common format, it is our hope that readers will be able to distinguish one type from the others within the same framework. Also, by including in the last chapter problems that arise in the investigation of a mass murder case, we hope to move the book into an expanded market of readers, the practitioners. This group of readers has often been overlooked by academics. Our position is that this is a grave mistake. There must be a blend of theory, research, and practice.

One never finishes a book such as this without the help of others. We are indebted to many people who have listened, helped, criticized (in a most gentle manner), and offered encouragement. This is the time to mention their names: David Rivers, Metro-Miami Police Department; Jay Whitt, Greensboro, North Carolina Police Department; Tom Harris, author (*Red Dragon* and the *Silence of the Lambs*); Drs. Gennaro Vito and Richard Tewksbury, University of Louisville; Lt. George Barret, Louisville Police Department; Dr. Steve Egger, Illinois State University at Springfield; Dr. Eric Hickey, University of California at Fresno (may his problem be solved with Rogaine—he is such a nice guy, and he needs this special blessing); Dr. Neil Haskell, forensic entomologist; Dr. Arpad Vass, forensic anthropologist; Lucy Davis, DNA expert; Deb Fraunfelter, Hocking College, Nelsonville, Ohio; Dr. Sally Hillsman, National Institute of Justice; Dr. Bernie McCarthy, University of Central Florida; Dr. David Fabianic, University of Central Florida; Jim Massie, Kentucky Department of Probation and Parole; Dr. Jack Levin, Northeastern University; Drs. Eddie Latessa, Jim Frank, and Lorraine Mazerolle, all of the University of Cincinnati; and Dr. Bob Langworthy, University of Alaska. We would also like to extend our thanks and appreciation to the following reviewers for their many helpful critiques of the manuscript: Donald G. Hanna, Cedarville College, Department of Criminal Justice; Lou Holscher, San Jose State University, College of Applied Sciences and Arts; and K. Lee Derr, Penn State University, School of Public Affairs. We are certain there are others, but please accept our regrets for not mentioning you.

Of course, no book reaches fuitition without the help of the family. Thanks.

R.M.H.
S.T.H.
2001

CHAPTER 1

Mass Murder in the United States

On Saturday, February 14, 1998, a 16-year-old boy was accused of killing five people. The young boy, who was a loner, liked to write poetry and play music, killed a mother, her three small children and the boy's 17-year-old half-brother. The police had no comment concerning a motive. The suspect's grandmother said that boy was upset because his half-brother was dating the murdered mother, who was 30 years old. The people in this small town in Noble, Illinois were shocked at the news.

On March 10, 1998, a lone gunman walked into his place of employment. He had just returned from a work-related stress disability leave. He hunted down and killed three supervisors inside the office complex of the state lottery office, and the lottery chief in the parking lot. Then the mass killer, Matthew Beck, age 35, killed himself. Fellow workers stated that he had been displeased that he had been passed over for promotions and that the lottery operations cheated the lottery players.

In November 1999, suspected gunman Bryan Uyesugi was arrested after allegedly killing seven Xerox employees. The motivation was unknown. He was under no threat of losing his job at the company. This was the worst mass killing in Xerox's history as well as in Hawaii's history.

On March 23, 1998, two young boys, Mitchell Johnson and Andrew Golden, opened fire on a playground of a middle school in Jonesboro, Arkansas. They killed four students: Paige Herring, Natalie Brooks, Brittany Varner, and Stephanie Johnson. A teacher, Shannon Wright, age 32, was also killed. The older boy had told several students the previous day that he was going to kill all the girls who had "broken up" with him. Even with that statement and with the boy pulling a knife on another boy in the school locker room the previous day, no one took the boy's remarks seriously until it was too late.

INTRODUCTION

Murder is a topic that has garnered the attention of most Americans. It appears that despite the drop in the sheer numbers and the ratio of people murdered, the American public is still interested in the topic of homicide. It remains one of the major social concerns and issues among old and young alike (Egger, 1997; Hickey, 1997; Holmes and Holmes, 1996, 1998a,b; Monahan, 1994).

This appetite for murder has been fed by the media (Jenkins, 1994; Lester, 1995). Various forms of the media have fueled the flame for the need to know more about the killers as well as what can be done to protect oneself from being a victim (Egger, 1997; Hickey, 1997). Television, for example, has a steady stream of programs in which murder is generally the central crime under investigation. *Law and Order*, *NYPD Blue*, and similar programs typically showcase a murder case that is resolved by the end of the hour. Movies such as *The Silence of the Lambs*, *Manhunter*, *Copy Cat*, *Seven*, and others, depict murder, especially serial murder, as a crime that is so common that it presents for each of us a real and present danger, as well as one not easily avoided.

On the other hand, mass murder has received relatively little attention in the media. Only when a major mass murder crime has been committed does the media alert the American public about the real danger that mass murder presents. The Oklahoma City bombing by Timothy McVeigh and Terry Nichols was a horrific crime and illustrated that anyone could be a victim of a mass murderer despite having absolutely no connection or relationship with the killer. The same could be said of the 1984 mass murder crime at the McDonald's restaurant in San Ysidro, California, although it received less fanfare and national attention. James Oliver Huberty killed lunchtime customers at the fast-food restaurant. He was then killed by a police sharpshooter.

Of the three types of *multicide*—mass murder, serial murder, and spree murder—mass murder usually receives the least amount of public attention (Holmes and Holmes, 1995, 1998a). Serial killers seem to attract the most media attention. Spree murderers commit their crimes in a relatively short period of time. The focus of their crimes is usually utilitarian, to silence any witnesses, and there are ongoing crimes of this nature. Mass murder comes to our attention less frequently than do spree crimes. Serial murder seems to be on the consciousness of most Americans on a continuing basis, whereas we think of mass murder only when there is a dramatic case that affects a large number of people. The intensity of the presentation of the case by the media is strong, but it is also quick to end (Holmes and Holmes, 1995).

For the purpose of this discussion, we adopt the following definitions (see Table 1.1):

- *Mass murder:* the killing of three or more people at one time and in one location.
- *Serial murder:* the killing of three or more people in more than a 30-day period with a significant cooling-off period between the murders. Serial killers may or not

be motivated by sexual impulses. For an in-depth examination of serial murder, we recommend the following books: *Serial Killers and Their Victims*, by Eric Hickey; *Serial Killers*, by Steve Egger; and *Serial Murder*, by Holmes and Holmes.

- *Spree murder:* the killing of three or more people usually within a 30-day period and typically during the course of another felony (such as a robbery).

Only when a high-profile mass murder crime occurs is there national media exposure. The crime is typically short-lived in the media (with the exception of the Oklahoma City bombing), and citizens soon forget the crime and the criminal. Relatives, friends, and relatives of the victims are left in remembrance of the deed (Holmes and Holmes, 1996).

In this book we examine the topic of mass murder and the various types of mass murderers. Doing research for this book, we were hindered by the lack of reliable information and academic research related directly to mass murder (Nisbett, 1993). Most of the data found dealt with felony homicide, domestic homicide, and serial murder. After more research has been completed, we may find that mass murder accounts for more killings and victims annually than does serial murder. Of the more than 20,000 victims who are murdered annually, we estimate that about 500 are victims of serial killers (Holmes and Holmes, 1995, 1998a). To examine this problem further, let us first look at the overall incidence of murder in the United States.

INCIDENCE OF MURDER IN THE UNITED STATES

The murder rate in the United States rose sharply from 1964 to 1974. For example the *Sourcebook on Criminal Justice Statistics, 1995* (Maguire and Pastore, 1996) reports that there were 7990 homicides in 1964. Ten years later, there were 18,532 murders. However, from 1984 to 1995, the murder rate did not changed dramatically. Table 1.2 contains the basic data for the number of murders.

From the information contained in Table 1.2, it is clear that the murder and manslaughter numbers have changed little since 1984. For example, in 1984 there

TABLE 1.1   Types of Multicide and Distinguishing Traits

Type	Number of Victims	Time Frame	Accompanying Felony?	Sexually Motivated?	Weapons Used
Serial	Three or more	More than 30 days	Usually not	Usually	Hands-on weapons
Mass	Three or more	Single episode	Usually not	No	Often weapons that kill from a distance
Spree	Three or more	Within 30 days	Yes, sometimes several felonies	No	Typically with hand guns, knives, etc.

TABLE 1.2   Number of Murders and Nonnegligent
             Manslaughters, 1984–1995

Year	Number
1984	16,689
1885	17,545
1886	19,257
1987	17,859
1988	18,269
1989	18,954
1990	20,045
1991	21,505
1992	22,540
1993	23,271
1994	22,076
1995	20,043

Source: Adapted from Maguire and Pastore (1996, Table 3.128).

were 16,689 murders and nonnegligent manslaughters. This number peaked in 1993; when there were 23,271. By 1995, the number had dropped to 20,043, the lowest it had been since the turn of the decade. How many of these acts were committed by mass killers? There is really no statistical method of determining the exact number. However, what is known is that many acts have been committed by mass killers whose crimes have been chronicled in the mass media.

The list of mass killers in Table 1.3 contains only the names of alleged mass killers and the total number of their victims. If one examines the chart using affinity and/or location, it is readily apparent that in the 1990s there have been more than 100 cases of mass murder.

To attempt to locate more accurate data, several federal resources were examined but without success. For example, the *Sourcebook on Criminal Justice Statistics* has no data on mass murders. However, it does contain a very interesting table listing victims of workplace violence. Of the 912 reported victims of homicide in the workplace, the majority were white males between the ages of 25 and 55. A majority (80 percent) of the victims were killed by shooting, but there is no way to determine how many victims were killed at one time and in one place. We can gather some of this information from less reliable sources, such as media reports. Such a flaw in the reporting procedure could lead one to wonder if mass murder is considered to be a social concern or problem.

We always instruct students to consider a social problem on the basis of four criteria. First, *is the situation undesirable?* Certainly, homicide is an undesirable act according to society's norms. There are few who would believe that it is permissible

TABLE 1.3   Alleged and Suspected Modern Mass Murderers, 1990s[a]

State	Murderer	Death Toll
Alabama	Jason Williams	Shot 3 family members and 1 other adult
	Joseph Akin	Allegedly killed 18 patients in a hospital
Alaska	Paul Ely, Jr.	Killed his wife and 2 children
	James Price	Killed 3 boarding house residents
Arizona	Shane Harrison	Killed 5 people in a robbery
	Norman Yazzie	Shot his 4 children
	Robert Smith	Killed 5 people in a beauty college
Arkansas	Mitchell Johnson	Killed 4 fellow students and a teacher
	Andrew Golden	Killed 4 fellow students and a teacher
	Damien Echols	Killed 3 young boys
	Jason Baldwin	Killed 3 young boys
	Jesse Misskelley	Killed 3 young boys
California	Frederick Davidson	Killed 3 members of his thesis committee
	Eric Houston	Killed 4 people at his former high school
	Arturo Suarez	Killed 4 people
	Sandi Nieves	Killed 4 children
	John Orr	Killed 4 people by arson
	Susan Eubanks	Killed her 4 children and herself
	Michael Perry	Killed 5 people, including his parents
	Joshua Jenkins	Killed 5 family members
	Jorjik Avanesian	Killed 7 family members
	Gian Ferri	Killed 6 in an attorney's office
	Leonardo Morita	Killed his wife, 3 children, and a maid
	Willie Woods	Shot 4 fellow workers
	Alan Winterbourne	Shot 5 people
	Dora Buenrostro	Killed her 3 children
	Christopher Green	Killed 4 at a post office
	Ronald Taylor	Killed 5 friends and relatives
Colorado	Eric Harris	Killed 13 at his high school
	Dylan Klebold	Killed 13 at his high school
	William Neal	Killed 3 women with an ax
	Albert Petrosky	Killed his wife, a shopper, and a police officer
Connecticut	Geoff Ferguson	Shot 5 people
	Errol Dehaney	Killed his wife and 2 children
	Matthew Beck	Killed 4 co-workers

TABLE 1.3 (Continued)

State	Murderer	Death Toll
Delaware	Richard Herr	Killed 3 fellow workers
Florida	James Pough	Shot 13 in an auto loan company
	Henry Carr	Killed 2 police officers and a young boy
	Miranda Shaw	Set fire to her 3 children and herself
	Curtis Windom	Shot his girlfriend and 2 adults
	Clifton McCree	Shot 5 co-workers
	David Vitaver	Killed his wife, son, and daughter
	Carl Brown	Shot 8 people in a machine shop
Georgia	Scott Heidler	Killed his foster parents and 2 children
Hawaii	Orlando Ganal	Shot 4 people, including his in-laws
	Bryan Uyesugi	Killed 7 fellow employees
Illinois	Lavern Ward	Killed his girlfriend and their 2 children
	Charles Smith	Killed his girlfriend and her 3 relatives
	Eric Matthews	Killed his wife, 2 ex-girlfriends, and his stepson
Indiana	John Stephenson	Shot 3 people
	Joseph Corcoran	Killed 6 people, including his brother
	John Ritzert	Shot his 3 children
Iowa	Gang Lu	Shot 5 college officials and college students
	Larry Buttz	Killed his wife, two children, and himself
Kentucky	Michael Brunner	Shot his girlfriend and her 2 children
	Robert Daigneau	Shot his wife and 3 strangers
	John Stephenson	Shot a husband, wife, and another man
	Michael Carneal	Killed 3 fellow students
	Jason Bryant	Killed 3 members of a family
	Michael Carneal	Killed 3 fellow students
	Natasha Cornett	Killed 3 members of a family
	Crystal Sturgill	Killed 3 members of a family
	Karen Howell	Killed 3 members of a family
	Dean Mullins	Killed 3 members of a family
	Joe Risner	Killed 3 members of a family
	Ronnie Sparks	Killed 3 backpackers
	Clay Shrout	Killed his father, mother, and 2 sisters
Louisiana	Antoinette Franks	Killed 4 patrons in a restaurant and a police officer
	Michael Fisher	Stabbed his mother, stepfather, and stepbrother
	Michael Perry	Killed 5 family members

TABLE 1.3 (Continued)

State	Murderer	Death Toll
Maryland	Mark Clark	Bombed his wife and 4 children
	Bruman Alvarez	Killed a doctor, his 3 daughters, and a housepainter
Massachusetts	Anthony Clemente	Killed 4 family members
	Damian Clemente	Killed 4 family members
	Peter Contos	Killed his girlfriend and their 2 children
	Mark Clark	Bombed his wife and 3 children
	Timothy Prink	Killed 4 family members
Michigan	Lawrence DeLisle	Drowned his 4 children
	Ilene Russell	Set a fire that killed 4 adults and 1 child
	Thomas McIvane	Shot 3 children
	Allen Griffin, Jr.	Shot 3 people at a bank
Minnesota	Paul Crawford	Shot 4 neighbors
	Khoua Her	Strangled her 6 children
	David Brown	Killed 4 family members
	James Schnick	Killed 7 family members
Mississippi	Ken Jones	Killed his wife and 4 co-workers
	Kenneth Tornes	Killed his wife and 4 co-workers
	Luke Woodham	Killed his mother and 2 students at a high school
Missouri	James Johnson	Killed 4 people
	Bruman Alvarez	Stabbed 5 people
	Mark Christeson	Killed a mother and 2 children
	Jesse Carter	Killed a mother and 2 children
	Jeffrey Sloan	Killed his parents and 2 brothers
Montana	Reginald Sublett	Killed his ex-girlfriend, their son, and 2 others
Nebraska	Marvin Nissen	Killed 3 women
	John Cotter	Killed 3 women
Nevada	Martin Garcia	Killed his 2 stepdaughters and a niece
New Hampshire	James Colbert	Strangled his wife and suffocated 3 daughters
	Carl Drega	Killed 4 people in his town
New Jersey	Joseph Harris	Shot 4 people in a post office
New Mexico	Stanley Secatero	Killed 4 relatives on a reservation
New York	Julio Gonzalez	Set a nightclub fire that killed 87 people
	Andrew Brooks	Shot his father and 3 men
	Colin Ferguson	Shot 6 people in a subway

TABLE 1.3   (Continued)

State	Murderer	Death Toll
	Michael Vernon	Killed 5 people in a shoe store
	Patrick Biller	Killed his wife and 3 children
	Roland Smith	Burned 7 people
	Michael Stevens	Killed his girlfriend's mother, sister, and stepfather
	Gary Evans	Killed 5 people
	Richard Timmons	Killed his wife and 2 children
North Carolina	James Davis	Killed 3 co-workers
	Jose Osorio	Killed 5 migrant workers
	Alonzo Osorio	Killed 5 migrant workers
Ohio	Kim Chandler	Shot her 3 children
	Joseph Lundgren	Shot 5 family members of a cult
	Richard Brand	Shot 5 family members of a cult
	Todd Hall	Killed 9 people in a fireworks store
	Gerald Clemons	Killed 3 people at his former workplace
Oklahoma	Timothy McVeigh	Killed 168 people in the federal building
	Terry Nichols	Killed 168 people in the federal building
	Danny Hooks	Killed 5 women in a crack house
Oregon	Girley Crum	Killed 3 adults and 2 children
	Ray DeFord	Killed 8 people by arson
	Kipland Kinkel	Killed his parents and students at his school
	Barry Loukaitas	Killed 3 fellow students
	David Whitson	Killed his wife and 3 children
Pennsylvania	David Freeman	Stabbed and beat to death his parents and brother
	Bryan Freeman	Stabbed and beat to death his parents and brother
	George Banks	Killed 9 family members
	Miguelina Estevez	Killed her 3 children and herself
	Robert Renninger	Killed his wife and 2 children
South Carolina	Fred Kornahrens	Killed his wife, her father, and his 2 children
	John Satterwhite	Killed his son and 3 stepchildren
Tennessee	Courtney Matthews	Shot 4 people in a Taco Bell
	David Housler	Shot 4 people in a Taco Bell
	Tony Carruthers	Killed 3 people
	James Montgomery	Killed 3 people
	Jason Bryant	Killed 3 members of a family
	Karen Hoill	Killed 3 members of a family

TABLE 1.3   (Continued)

State	Murderer	Death Toll
	Daryl Holton	Killed his ex-wife and 3 children
	Everett Cobb	Killed his ex-wife, her new husband, and a friend
Texas	George Hennard	Shot 22 people in a restaurant
	James Mankins	Killed 5 people at a restaurant
	James Simpson	Killed his wife, boss, and 3 co-workers
	Steven Renfro	Killed his girlfriend, aunt, and neighbor
	Robert Coulson	Killed his adopted parents and 3 others
	Coy Wesbrook	Killed his wife and 3 others
	Virgil Martinez	Killed his wife, 2 children, and a friend
Vermont	Richard Stevens	Killed 3 people near a college campus
Virginia	Douglas Buchanan	Killed his father, stepmother, and 2 stepbrothers
Washington	Timothy Black III	Shot 3 women and an unborn fetus
	Barry Loukaitas	Killed his teacher and 2 fellow students
	Martin Pang	Killed 4 firefighters
	Alex Barany, Jr.	Killed a husband, wife, and their 2 children
	David Anderson	Killed a husband, wife, and their 2 children
	Sam Lau	Killed his wife and 2 children
West Virginia	Ricky Brown	Killed 5 children
	Barbara Brown	Killed 5 children
	Janette Abler	Killed 5 children
	Mark Storm	Killed his wife, brother, and 2 children

[a]In some cases the murderer may not have been charged with all the victims listed because of the expense and lack of direct evidence to assure a conviction. In some cases, for example, a person may be charged with only one murder but be thought by the police and the courts to be responsible for the others. Also, there are a few cases where the arrested have not yet gone to trial.

to murder indiscriminately people who have no relationship to the killer and who in no way contributed to the killer's own victimization. Next, the act *affects a significant number of people.* This is a tricky determination: How many people have to be mass murder victims before the number is considered significant by those who live in our society? The point here is that no baseline number is required for mass murder to be considered a social problem; the number will vary from one person to the next. There is no doubt, however, that when McVeigh and Nichols bombed the federal building in Oklahoma City and 168 people were killed, that single act brought the problem of mass murder to widespread attention and affected a significant number of people.

Next, a social problem must *be able to be remedied*. Can we do this for mass murder any more than we can for serial murder? This is a difficult question to answer with any certainty.

Finally, a social problem *must be remediable through collective social action*. In other words, for mass murder to be considered a social problem, the act that must be remedied by other acts by those in society who have the power and authority to do so. One person cannot solve the problem of mass murder; it must be done on a national level. How? This is a question that is addressed in this book.

Despite not knowing the exact number of people who fall victim to mass killers, it is usually found that a mass killer murders intimates as well as strangers (Levin and Fox, 1985). There are some mass killers, the family annihilators, who kill spouses or partners, children, and even family pets. There is another type of mass killer who may kill people they know if only on a superficial basis, such as people who work in the same building or plant as does the killer. This has been seen in various cases, such as that of Richard Farley, who killed several people at a computer company where he had recently been terminated. He killed them as one way to get the attention of his love object, who had spurned his amorous advances. Several sets of relationships may exist for a mass killer, and the examination of one type of relationship would probably not give a researcher a true indication of the extent of the problem.

In Table 1.4, for example, we list the number of murders and nonnegligent manslaughters in 1995, together with the relationship of the murderer and victims.

As we see, however, the relationship between killer and victim still does not aid us in determining how many of the killings involve mass murder. Although the family may well be "the cradle of violence," more than 50 percent of the victims of murder and nonnegligent manslaughter were strangers or the relationship between the victim and killer was not unknown. Of course, some of those in the "unknown" category may be family members or other types of "significant others," but there is, at present, no way to determine the relationship, if one does exist. In the cases that are known, husbands and wives account for less than 5 percent of all murder victims. Can some of these victims also be victims of a mass murder in which, for example, the wife was killed together with two children? The data available do not yield such information. Moreover, there does not appear to be a reliable source of such information.

CONCLUSION

In this chapter we have painted a dreary picture of the state of affairs regarding accumulating accurate data on the incidence of mass murder. The federal government, the repository of much knowledge, especially statistics, does not appear to be a reliable source for the information needed. One available source is that of

TABLE 1.4 Murders and Nonnegligent Manslaughters Known to the Police by Victim–Offender Relationship, United States, 1995

Relationship of Victim	Total	Percent
Husband	267	1.3
Wife	732	3.6
Mother	114	0.5
Father	148	0.7
Son	281	1.4
Daughter	226	1.1
Brother	124	0.6
Sister	24	0.1
Other family	382	1.9
Acquaintance	5,347	26.7
Friend	584	2.9
Boyfriend	191	0.9
Girlfriend	482	2.4
Neighbor	175	0.9
Employee	7	0.03
Employer	18	0.09
Stranger	3,036	15.1
Unknown	7,905	39.4
	20,043	

Source: Adapted from Maguire and Pastore (1996, Table 3.127).

news clippings, newscasts, and the like, but we hasten to add that this is a most unreliable method; certainly, many cases will be missed. However, it is the one method that can be utilized that will secure some of the information needed. Unreliable as it is, sometimes this is all we have and we must use it while acknowledging the obvious shortcomings.

While realizing the shortcomings in gathering data for examination, let us move on to the second chapter, a short history of mass murder in the United States. Again, knowing that the true extent of mass murder is unknown, it is our opinion that the true significance of any social problem, including mass murder, cannot be measured in numbers alone. What we do know is sufficient to justify not only our interest in this form of homicide but also dedication to an effort to reduce the numbers of mass murder acts and thus reducing the number of victims and other collateral sufferers.

Discussion Questions

1. What sources or outlets have increased interest in the crime of murder and the criminals who commit it? What effect can or has the increased attention being paid to murder had on American society?

2. What are the three types of multicide? How is each similar to or different from the others? Why is it important to distinguish among the three types?

3. Why is the "story life" of the crimes of a mass murderer typically short-lived? What accounts for the difference in the interest of the media and the general public between mass and serial murderers?

4. What four elements should be considered when determining if a phenomenon is a social problem. How can these be applied to the study of mass murder?

5. Given that official government statistics do not accurately record the number of victims or actual persons thought to be mass murderers, how do you think we can remedy the problem on a national basis?

CHAPTER 2

History of Mass Murder in the United States

On October 2, 1997, Timothy Prink shot and killed his adopted parents, an adopted daughter, and his adopted grandmother. He said, "What have I done? They're going to put me away for a long time."

On February 11, 1998, two teenagers charged in the slaying of a Missouri woman and her two children were captured in California after a detective recognized them from wanted posters. Mark Christeson, 18, and Jesse Carter, 17, were arrested in Blythe, California. The bodies of Susan Brouck, 36, her daughter, Adrian, 12, and a son, Kyle, 9, were found in a farm pond near their trailer.

On March 19, 1998, a man who was not pleased that his father married so quickly after his mother had died was executed for the murder of his father, stepmother, and two stepbrothers. Douglas Buchanan, Jr., was executed by lethal injection for these murders, committed on September 15, 1987.

INTRODUCTION

Many believe that mass murder is a relatively recent social phenomenon. This is untrue. There have been cases of mass murder since early in our country's history. Many of these acts of multicide are unrecorded. Perhaps many early victims of such crimes were the underclass of the society at the time. We do not dismiss their suffering or victimization, but it is more recent history that we are concerned with, the period since the early 1960s.

No case better illustrates the beginning of the interest in mass murder than that of Charles Whitman. Mass killings by other killers followed: Richard Speck, James Oliver Huberty, Joseph Wesbecker, and others. In this section, two selected cases of mass murder are examined. Commentary is added to demonstrate social and community concerns that accompany such tragic acts. The case of Charles Whitman was one of the first to alert the nation to the problem of mass killers (Levin and Fox, 1985, p. 16). The second case, one of the most recent, illustrates mass murder by a youth, Michael Carneal, age 14, who went into his high school in December 1997 and killed three classmates and wounded four others.

CHARLES WHITMAN: THE KILLER FROM THE TOWER*

On July 31, 1966, Charles Whitman picked up his wife from her part-time summer job in downtown Austin, Texas. At approximately 12:30 P.M, he dropped her off at their apartment. He then drove to his mother's home. He had already written two notes regarding his plans to kill his mother, his wife, and a number of innocent victims. In the first note he stated that he would take his mother's life. He described his love for his mother and his hatred for his father. He then proceeded to his mother's apartment, where he stabbed her five times, shot her once in the back of the head, and broke her left hand. He left the following note on the night-stand next to her bed.

> To whom it may concern,
>
> I have just taken my mother's life. I am very upset over having done it. However, I feel that if there is a heaven, she is definately [sic] there now. And if there is no life after, I have relieved her from her suffering here on earth. The intense hatred I feel for my father is beyond description. My mother gave that man the best 25 years of her life and because she finally took enough of his beatings, humiliation, degration [sic], and tribulations, that I am sure no one but she and he will ever know—to leave him. He has chosen to treat her like a slut that you would bed down with, accept her favors and then throw a pitance [sic] in return.
>
> I am truly sorry that this is the only way I could see to relieve her sufferings, but I think it was best.
>
> Let there be no doubt in our minds, I loved that woman with all my heart.
>
> If there exists a God, let him understand my actions and judge me accordingly,
>
> Charles Whitman

After killing his mother, he drove home and stabbed his wife four times (some believe, one stab for each of the four years they had been together). She was apparently asleep. There was no sign of a struggle.

He also typed another note on that same night.

> I don't quite understand what it is that compels me to type this letter. Perhaps it is to leave some vague reason for the actions I have just recently performed. I don't really understand myself these days. I was supposed to be an average, reasonable and intelligent young man. However, lately (I don't recall when it started) I have been a victim of many unusual and irrational thoughts. These thoughts constantly recur and it requires a tremendous mental effort to concentrate on useful and progressive tasks. In March, when my parents made a physical break I noticed a great deal of stress. I consulted a Dr. Cochrum at the University Health Center and asked him to recommend someone that I could consult with about some psychiatric disorders I felt I had....
>
> Charles J. Whitman

---

*Much of this information concerning Whitman was adapted from Lavergne (1997).

On the next day at noon, Whitman climbed the tower at the University of Texas. He transported a green duffel bag on a cart up the elevators of the University of Texas clock tower. The bag, labeled "Lance Cpl. C. J. Whitman," contained, among other things, water and gasoline, rope, binoculars, canteens, spray deodorant, toilet paper, a machete, a Bowie knife, a hatchet, a 6mm Remington bolt-action rifle (with a 4× power Leupold telescopic sight), a .35-caliber Remington rifle, a Galesi-Brescia pistol, a .357 Magnum Smith & Wesson revolver, a .30-carbine, a 12-gauge sawed-off shotgun (which he had purchased earlier that day), shot magazines, and over 700 rounds of ammunition.

Arriving on the thirtieth floor of the tower, Whitman first killed Edna Townsley, a receptionist at the facility. He beat her in the head and then shot her to death. From atop the tower, Whitman fired onto the campus grounds. The shooting lasted almost two hours. Arranging his time for the onslaught to begin when classes were breaking, Whitman killed from a distance. He shot Claire Wilson, a young mother-to-be. She survived the shot but later gave birth to a stillborn baby. The baby had been fatally wounded by the bullet from Whitman. He also killed Thomas Eckman, age 19, who had rushed to aid Ms. Wilson. Robert Boyle was killed as well as Roy Dell Schmidt, a technician who had just completed a repair assignment. Thomas Ashton, a 22-year-old Peace Corps trainee, Paul Sonntag and Claudia Rutt (friends), Harry Walchuk, and Thomas Karr were among some of the 15 dead victims.

Three police officers, along with a civilian, made their way through underground tunnels to the tower. At the top, they shot Whitman to death. In a personal interview, one officer said that one man shot Whitman and that Whitman moved. The officer then shot him again to ensure that he was dead.

A medical autopsy was completed on Whitman to determine if there was a tumor or some other form of medical abnormality that would account for this propensity to violence. A brain tumor was found. Whether this was a direct contributing factor in these deaths was never determined.

Charles Whitman was born in 1941. In 1966, the 25-year-old ex-Marine, devoted to his family, was devastated when his parents decided to divorce. He began to act oddly, breaking into fits of violence and complaining of severe headaches. He sought psychiatric counseling, but his mother and his wife attributed his behavioral change to the stress of a heavy class load. At the University of Texas at Austin on July 31, prior to killing his mother and his wife, Whitman wrote a note that read: "I am prepared to die. After my death, I wish an autopsy on me to be performed to see if there is any mental disorder." He added in another part of the note, "Life is not worth living."

Conclusion of the Charles Whitman Case. Although never truly understanding Whitman's motivation to kill, most people view him with a sense of infamy. Those closest to him were not in a position to offer any insight, and his father, who has since died, was a person whom Whitman held in extremely low esteem. The father refused interviews, but those who knew Whitman knew that the son and the father were estranged.

The effects of the Whitman case lingered for years. The tower from which Whitman killed and wounded innocent victims was closed in 1975 because of a number of suicides, people jumping to their death from the 231-foot tower. Only recently has the University of Texas decided to reopen the tower.

Let us now examine a case of mass murder very different in motivation and anticipated gain from that of Whitman. It is also different in scope: Whitman killed 15, Carneal killed three.

MICHAEL CARNEAL: A YOUTHFUL MASS KILLER

On Monday morning, December 1, 1997, a 14-year-old boy, a freshman at Heath High School in western Kentucky, went to school early. Inside his coat he carried five guns and 600 rounds of ammunition. The weapons and the ammunition were allegedly stolen from a neighbor. Entering the school, he went toward a small group of students who were at school early for a Bible study session. He placed earplugs in his ears, pulled a handgun from his backpack, and shot eight students; three died (Table 2.1).

Carneal told a few classmates the week before that something "big" was soon going to happen at school. None of the young people apparently took his boasts seriously. None notified school officials and remembered Carneal's statement only after the incident. One classmate, Ben Strong, said: "He told me he was going to do something, but he wouldn't tell me what it was....But he told me not to be there, because, you know, we're friends." Another student, Alison Bell, said: "He just stood there and fired....He didn't move. He just stood in the same spot" ("No warning: 'he just stood there and fired,'" *Courier-Journal*, Louisville, KY, December 2, 1997, p. A11).

TABLE 2.1   Victims of Mass Killer Michael Carneal

Name	*Age*
WOUNDED	
Kelly Hard	16
Hollan Holm	14
Melissa Jenkins	15
Craig Keene	15
Shelly Schaberg	17
MURDERED	
Nicole Hadley	14
Jessica James	17
Kayce Steger	15

Immediately following the shooting, students stood there motionless. After the initial shock passed, there was screaming. The young people starting running through the hallways. The school principal, Bill Bond, reported that when he stepped out of his office, he saw students running and screaming. He noted five students lying on the hallway floor. He said he saw blood everywhere. Ben Strong, the student, said that about 10 shots were fired before he realized what had happened. "Then I seen [sic] some people fall, and I seen [sic] blood….And I ran up to him and I kind of pushed him against the wall. And he was, like, 'I can't believe I did this.' Because he shot one of his friends who was just a few feet away. Because he wasn't aiming at any person. And he said, 'Kill me now,' or something like that. I was just telling him to be calm, drop the gun, whatever. And he just kind of slouched down and dropped the gun" (ibid.).

People at the scene identified Michael Carneal as the shooter. He gave himself up at the school. Because he was arrested as a juvenile, his name was not initially released by the press. Only after his case was waived by the juvenile court to the adult court was his name released for public notice.

Heath is a small town with one stoplight. It is within a few miles of the largest town in western Kentucky, Paducah. People in this small community were horrified at the crime and were equally at a loss to explain what had happened and what would cause this young boy to commit such a crime. Close neighbors were certainly at a loss to explain it. The neighbors of the Carneals all said that the family was well liked and respected in the area. The father is an attorney and has been practicing law for the last 20 years. In talking with a friend who lives in Heath, he said the family is the all-American type. He knew the killer and could not understand the attack. He said that the boy appeared to be a nice young man and was at a loss for words of explanation.

There appears to be no clear and concise reason for the mass murder by Michael Carneal. He was thought by those in his community to come from a stable and good family. His mother and father were married. Michael himself enjoyed a favorable reputation. Michael and his father did things together, such as playing golf. They also played board games in the comfortable home that the family had built barely six years earlier. But as the investigation continued, neighbors started to remember things about this young man. Jim Adams, a reporter for the *Courier-Journal*, conducted a series of interviews with people in Heath. The neighbors recalled that Michael was seen as an immature youth but not a troublemaker. He was thought to be shy and withdrawn from many of the other young people in this semirural area. They described him as an intelligent youth who enjoyed playing with his computer; making videos with a friend, a young boy who lived next door to the Carneals; listening to heavy metal music; and with a new and emerging interest in wearing black clothing. One neighbor stated that she noticed that Michael was becoming more secretive and rebellious. The authorities in the community were quick to add that they were not aware of any cult involvement.

In seeking some explanation for the act of mass murder, some alluded to the possibility that Michael was a victim of incessant teasing by other boys in the high school. There was also a possibility, according to some, that others might be involved in this mass murder, including satanic and black magic involvement, and that Michael may have been influenced by a violent movie he had seen recently, *Menace II Society* (J. Adams, "Teen 'fidgety,' not troublesome," *Courier-Journal*, Louisville, KY, December 2, 1997, pp. A1, A11; J. Adams, "Sheriff thinks boy shared shooting plan," *Courier-Journal*, Louisville, KY, December 4, 1997, pp. A1, A10). The parents were not giving interviews at the time; they did tell a family spokesperson that they were sincerely sorry for the victims and the families. Their minister reported the father to have said that as hurt and devastated as they are personally over this, they are just as hurt and devastated over the loss the community has suffered (J. Adams, "Grieving town asks 'Why?'" *Courier-Journal*, Louisville, KY, December 3, 1997, pp. A1, A8).

By the end of the week, the bodies of the three students were buried. Two thousand people from the small community, local and state politicians, and others, including the Heath High School band, were present. Three white caskets of the three slain young women were in front of the church pews. The caskets were open until the start of the burial service. The caskets chosen permitted their friends to sign their names or leave messages on them. By the time of the burial, the three caskets were inscribed with hundreds of messages from fellow students, friends, and family members.

In a rare sense of forgiveness, the community has not expressed a message of rage toward Michael or his family over what happened to three children in their community. The citizens have expressed forgiveness to Michael and to members of his family. The reports have uniformly reported that although no one dismisses the gravity of what has happened with the deaths of their most prized possession, their children, they have forgiven Michael. This is not to say that they condone what he had done—this will never happen—but the families all believe that they have to move to the process of mending.

Michael Carneal is just starting his experience with the criminal justice system. He was originally charged as a juvenile. However, Kentucky law permits a juvenile to be charged as an adult when a weapon is used in the course of a homicide. His case was transferred to the adult court system in Kentucky.

Some good has arisen from this case. One of the victims, Nicole Hadley, talked with her parents only a short time before she died. She wanted to contribute her organs to help others in case she died. One man, Thomas Hereford, received the lungs of the young woman. Another unidentified patient received her heart. Her liver, kidney, and pancreas were also donated to patients who needed the organs to live.

One victim who did survive the attack was Melissa Jenkins. However, she will spend the rest of her life paralyzed by a spinal cord injury. Detective Carl Baker of the local sheriff's department said that there was little chance that the young woman would ever walk again, according to medical authorities. He remarked that she is currently undergoing physical therapy and would probably be confined to a wheelchair for the rest of her life (personal interview, March 3, 1998).

Representatives of newspapers, and of radio and TV stations, as well as interested citizens, were at the scene. For three days the headlines announced every new development in this heinous crime. Community leaders were outraged. They called for school officials to develop a plan to make the school safe for students. They insisted that technology be in place that would detect weapons brought into the school by disgruntled students, teachers, or other people bent on mass murder or other forms of physical assault. The local police were also placed in a reactive mode. They were stationed at the high school as well as at other schools in the community in case a copycat slayer in their community decided to kill more students and teachers. But within a week after the burials, the media moved out of Heath and life has returned to relative normalcy. Political pontification by prosecutors and defense attorneys no longer appears on the front pages; they are hidden on the inside of the paper, in the daily news. Newscasters only rarely remark on the case, and then only in passing. People in this small town with one stop light in western Kentucky will never forget Michael Carneal and his victims, but the event will soon become a distant memory that can be recalled only with some deliberation. This is true of most mass killings and of newsworthy events in general.

Almost a year after the shooting, Carneal finally went to court. To avoid a long and expensive trial, the Commonwealth of Kentucky accepted a plea of guilty but mentally ill. The teenager was sentenced to an adult prison for 25 years without the possibility of parole. This news item appeared in a small article buried in the middle of the first section of the paper and was the fifth story on the TV newscast the night of the sentencing, in contrast to the case's earlier prominence in the front of many newspapers and as the lead story on the nightly news.

But the Carneal mass murder case is not over. In December 1998, the families of the slain three victims sued 45 defendants. In their lawsuit the parents stated that some of Carnel's friends knew that he had guns and had on occasion taken the guns to school. Six juveniles were accused in the lawsuit of conspiring and encouraging Carneal to commit the crime. The parents of Michael Carneal were also named as defendants. The suit alleged that his parents should have known that Michael was dangerous but did nothing to deter him or provide psychological services. School administrators and members of the board of education in this small county were also named as defendants. The position taken was that the board and school administrators should have developed a plan for such an occurrence. Some teachers were also included in the lawsuit, alleging that the teachers should have informed the school principal and others at the school concerning the violent content of papers that Michael submitted as schoolwork.

There was no mention of an exact amount of money. The parents have stated publicly that the lawsuit is not about money; rather, it is a "force" demanding policy development designed to preclude another case of mass murder in the school.

OTHER MASS KILLERS

There have been many other mass killers in U.S. history. Table 1.3 attests to the sheer numbers of the killers that we have discovered in our research. Several of these killers are highlighted in the chapters that follow. Jeffrey MacDonald, John List, and Ronald Gene Simmons are discussed as examples of family annihilators. Each of these killers was responsible for the death of members of his own family. Many of us remember the case of Jeffrey MacDonald. The Green Beret claimed that three hippies came into his home on the military base and stabbed his wife and two children to death. John List killed his wife, one daughter, and two sons and then disappeared, only to be found by law enforcement personnel years later. Ronald Gene Simmons, a retired Air Force sergeant, killed not only his immediate family but also members of his extended family. Other mass killers will be discussed in the context of their crimes: Willie Woods, David Burke, James Simpson, Joseph Wesbecker, and others.

Possibly the most infamous case of mass murder is the Oklahoma City bombing case of Timothy McVeigh and Terry Nichols. Ideological mass killers are also discussed, including David Koresch and Jim Jones. Jones's case occurred in the 1970s; other cases of this type are more recent. The case of the Heaven's Gate followers and the mass suicide directed by their leader, Do or Doe (Marshall Applewhite), is a perfect example of mass murder by suggestion or "religious" commandment.

A few mass murder cases remain unsolved. One is the Tylenol case, a case of mass murder performed by tampering with medicine that was purchased over the counter. Other examples of the set-and-run mass killer have been solved easily, as was the case with Julio Gonzalez, who set fire to the Happy Land Social Club in the Bronx, New York, in 1990. Eighty-seven people died in that mass murder. Although the intent may have been to frighten his girlfriend, the fact is that more than four score victims were killed—that is mass murder.

The disgruntled citizen mass murderer is a type that has been in our society for years. This fact is exemplified by cases of mass murder committed by such killers as Hubert de la Tore in the early 1980s. Looking at other cases, such as that of George Hennard at Luby's restaurant in Texas, Patrick Purdy in California, and James Oliver Huberty at McDonald's in San Ysidro, California, are examined. Other mass killers are out of touch with reality and mentally ill. These types of mass killers are placed in the psychotic mass killer category. Priscilla Ford is such an example.

The point is that mass killers are a danger that have been part of the killing scene in the United States for years. They are not new or indigenous to the United States. The names of mass killers are perhaps not as well known (with few exceptions), but their acts present a real and present danger. The danger posed by these types of killers will continue to be a part of our cultural ethos.

CONCLUSION

In the examination of mass killers in the last several years, it is apparent that in the latter part of the twentieth century, more mass murderers have been uncovered. Early mass killers, such as Howard Unruh, were such an uncommon occurrence that most Americans gave little attention to their actions. Perhaps one reason for this was that the reporting system of our country at that time was meager. Only within the last two decades has the reporting system become sophisticated and the reporting more reliable so that we are finally in a position to realize that mass murder is a problem that deserves serious attention from both the academic and law enforcement perspectives. It accounts for a substantial number of innocent victims but cannot be measured simply by the number of people involved.

Mass killers have been with us in this society for a long time, and there is no reason to believe that the numbers of such murders will diminish in the near or even the distant future. It is a fatal phenomenon that will undoubtedly stay with us. The mindset of all types of mass murderers, the implications of this for society at large, and the potential dangers posed to those who are potentially at risk certainly deserve examination.

Discussion Questions

1. What case of mass murder in recent history alerted the nation to the problem of the mass killer? Where did this incident occur, and what do we know about this offender's motives?

2. If Whitman expressed such love and devotion for his mother, why would he have taken her life in such a brutal manner? Why do you feel he felt the need to break her hand?

3. It is believed that there are a number of motivational factors behind the acts of Charles Whitman (e.g., hatred for father, brain tumor, stress, etc.). However, what pressing issues could compel an otherwise normal 14-year-old to kill a number of his friends and classmates? Why do you believe that Michael Carneal chose the group that he did? Could the incident in Heath, Kentucky have been prevented? How?

4. Why do you believe that there has been an increase in the number (or awareness of the number) of mass murderers in the United States during the past 20 years? What ramifications does or may this have on the prevalence of mass murders in the future?

CHAPTER 3

Mass Murder: Theory and Types

In 1996, in Harrodsburg, Kentucky, Robert Daigneau, age 45, fatally shot his wife and three others in a rage over the failure of his marriage. The witnesses stated that he carefully opened fire on his wife and three innocent bystanders who were in the car with her. The friends said that he was very jealous and thought that his wife was seeing another man. As a local police officer said: "He was a walking time bomb."

In Ankeny, Iowa, in 1996, Larry Buttz killed his wife Delane, 38, and their children, Ryan, 15, and Lindsey, age 12. He had been charged with domestic violence only a month before. After he killed his family, he killed himself.

In 1998, two teenagers killed five people. Then one of the juveniles killed the other. The survivor, age 17, was not identified because of his age. The police said that the killers killed two young boys, then went to another home and killed three other people. The motive in this case of mass murder is unknown.

INTRODUCTION

There is a general misunderstanding concerning mass murder. Often, the terms *mass murder* and *serial murder* are interchanged. For example, in the book jacket of Michaud and Aynesworth's book, *The Only Living Witness* (1983), Ted Bundy is called a mass murderer on the back cover of the book jacket. Ted Bundy was a *serial killer*, one who kills three people or more over a period of time, usually more than 30 days. Other times, the term *spree killer* is used—it then becomes all the more confusing. There are, however, fundamental differences between mass murder and serial murder (Holmes and Holmes, 1998a). The basic motivations, anticipated gains, victim selectivity, methods of murder, and other vital elements are unique to each type of multicide. Even within the different types of mass murder, we shall see that the loci of motivations and the anticipated gains, as well as the process of victim selection, are different from one type of mass killer to the other.

The purpose of this chapter is to examine a typology of mass killers as well as a selected theory of homicide related to mass murder. First, let us gather some basic information toward an understanding of mass murder.

WHAT IS MASS MURDER?

The intricacies of mass murder preclude a simple definition and thus a complete understanding. Mass murder has several definitions. The one that has been accepted most widely is "the willful killing of a number of people at one time and in one place." The baseline number that is generally agreed upon by most is three, (Hickey, 1997; Holmes and DeBurger, 1985, 1988; Holmes and Holmes, 1993, 1998b). Dietz defines mass murder as "the willful injuring of five or more persons of whom three are killed by a single offender in a single incident" [italics added] (1986, p. 480). Of course, the more limitations one places in the definitions, the fewer the mass killings that occur. For example, in Dietz's definition, five people have to be injured, two of whom do not die. It is difficult to understand why that nonfatal number is integral to the definition. Should it not be the number of victims fatally injured that is the necessary total for an adequate numerical qualification of mass murder? Of course, there are others who believe that it is necessary for more than three people to be the fatally injured. Why not set four as a baseline number? The answer to this question is not clear. In this book we yield to experts in the academic community, such as Hickey, Egger, and others, who offer a baseline number of three.

A potential mass murder scenario is further complicated by cases in which only two die. Does efficient emergency medical care in a potential mass murder case where lives are saved, and fewer than three people are fatally injured, reduce the number of mass killers as well as victims of mass murderers? It appears to be so. Various "statistical games" can be played by those who wish to debate numbers, but let us not get bogged down in such a debate, thus failing to understand the scope of the mass murder problem.

We believe that ordinarily, mass murder will occur at one time and in one place or location. Witness the recent case of Clifton McCree, age 41, in Fort Lauderdale. This one-time employee of the city's beach-cleanup crew was terminated from his job. City records indicate that he was fired from his unskilled position because of (1) his failure to pass a drug test, (2) harassment, (3) threatening his fellow workers, and (4) being rude to the public. The employees at the department had informed their supervisors that McCree was dangerous and should be watched. On February 9, 1996, he returned to his former place of employment with two guns. He shot to death five workers and critically wounded a sixth. McCree then turned the gun on himself and committed suicide. All the killings took place at one time and in one location. The motivation to kill was never truly determined. The killer left a suicide note, but the contents of the note were never disclosed. Some workers believed that the killings were racially motivated. McCree, a husband and father of two children, was black, and all the victims were white.

In another case, the kill site was not a single physical location. The case of Carl Drega, age 67, reflects the problem of demanding that the murder location be confined to one site.

Case Study

A News Account of the Drega Mass Murder Scene

August 19, 1997—2:40 P.M.

The three-hour havoc caused by Carl Drega of Columbia, a man lost in his own senseless rage, started at 2:40 p.m. on Tuesday, August 19.

Two weeks prior to their last day of duty, Troopers Scott Phillips and Leslie Lord discussed Carl Drega's 1974 Dodge truck. They determined it to be unsafe and unregisterable and decided that the next time either one of them saw the vehicle on the road it would be grounded with its license plates removed.

When Scott entered the parking lot of LaPerle's IGA on Route 3 in Colebrook he spotted Carl Drega's vehicle and called Leslie for assistance. He knew from a previous incident with Mr. Drega that the man would make his duty hard. To Scott's surprise, Drega quickly jumped from his vehicle shooting. The rifle scattered several rounds into Scott's legs. Although he was disabled, Scott returned fire until he emptied his revolver, but Drega was protected by a bullet-proof vest.

Leslie arrived and pulled his cruiser close to Drega's truck. Immediately, Drega began firing at Leslie as he backed up his car and threw it into drive. The car never moved. "Lucky" Lord took a fatal shot to his head.

Not done with his carnage at the IGA, Drega went back after Scott, who by this time lay in a nearby field behind the Green Mountain Snack Bar. He stood over the trooper and fired more shots, point blank, with a 9mm sidearm. He then went back to Leslie and fired more rounds at him as well.

Colebrook police converged onto the scene and took cover. Taking slow, even paces Drega calmly walked over to Scott's police cruiser and climbed inside. He drove away heading south on Route 3 and passed *News and Sentinel* reporter Claire Lynch-Knapper near the Brooks Chevrolet dealership in route to the IGA. It must be said here that Lance Walling and Albert Riff, among other employees at the IGA, reacted quickly and bravely, gathering customers outside the parking lot and inside the building into a safe place.

The *Sentinel* crew was putting the week's issue of the newspaper together when a voice came on the scanner reporting there was shooting at the IGA. Several gathered in the front office to listen to the scanner, including attorney and judge Vickie Bunnell. Then a voice came on again saying that an officer was down. Reporter Claire Lynch-Knapper grabbed her camera, jumped into her truck and headed for IGA, unknowingly passing Drega on Route 3 in Scott Phillip's cruiser headed toward the *Sentinel*.

Jana saw Drega pull up in the cruiser, saw him get out with a gun, and yelled, "My God he's got a gun. Everybody run." Vickie ran for Susan, and said, "It's Drega, run." She had been in fear of Drega for a long time. She had been a Columbia Selectmen and he had a long-standing grudge against the selectmen of Columbia. He had threatened her and she had resorted to carrying a gun around with her.

Vickie headed through her front office door leading to the *Sentinel* back door, pushing Susan in front of her. In a strong, calm, authoritative voice, she told the startled *Sentinel* crew, "There's a man with a gun, get out."

Gil had attempted to lock the front door but didn't make it in time. He retreated, locked the *Sentinel* inner door, and got into a corner as far out of sight as he could. Jana ran to the rear exit, shouting a warning for people to get out. Dennis was headed toward the front office and met Vivien, asking what was going on. Vivien replied, "There's a man with a gun." He immediately turned around and ran out the door. Gil Short, Vivien Towle, and Jeannette Ellingwood remained inside.

Jana ran across the parking lot around the front of Ducret's Sporting Goods. She could hear bullets hitting the building. She hid behind the building, then decided that wasn't safe and crossed the street to Dicken's Hair Salon.

Susan Sambito and Chandra Coviello also ran across the parking lot towards Ducret's, with Vickie close on their heels. Susan and Chandra made it through the back door of Ducret's with the sound of bullets thudding into the garage door above them. They didn't know that Vickie hadn't made it, but had been shot down in a parking lot just before reaching safety.

Photographer Leith Jones also ran across the parking lot but veered left, trying to reach his car. He passed the first car and was next to the second when shots rang out. "I thought they were aimed at me," said Leith.

Susan Zizza went out the back door with the others and thinking that she only had a few seconds, passed Dennis' car which was always parked close to the building and crawled between the rear wheels of a truck behind Dennis' vehicle. Unknown to all of them, the killer had not entered the *Sentinel* building but had run along the side of the building, and was there waiting at the corner of the building for Vickie to come out.

Just as Susan ducked under the car, she heard shots and saw Vickie fall to her left. To the right, only a car's length away, she saw Dennis and Drega coming around the corner of the *Sentinel* building struggling with the rifle.

According to Jeannette Ellingwood, as Drega began shooting, Dennis rushed through the rear door and grabbed Drega by the shoulders. They wrestled on the hood of Jeannette's car, but Dennis was unable to get complete control of the six-foot four-inch 230-pound man or his high assault rifle.

As they struggled around the corner with both their hands on the weapon, "the assailant gave a huge jerk on the muzzle end of the gun," said Leith, who was also watching the brief battle in horror from the parking lot, "and he broke Dennis' grip. He turned the weapon on Dennis and fired two shots. I don't know if the first shot hit Dennis, but he second one did, and Dennis went down."

Matt Rosi and John Brunault were visiting at the counter of Ducret's Sporting Goods with Richard Paquette and Dave Robidas when the women came through the back door. Phil Ducret arrive shortly afterward. The men in Ducret's had heard about the shooting at LaPerle's IGA almost the same time the shots outside their building began. They had armed themselves, thinking there was a second gunman.

Matt and John went out the back door, but had to dive to the floor of the garage as more bullets went over their heads. When the shooting stopped, said Karen Lamontagne, another witness to these events, the men in Ducret's spread out around the *Sentinel* creating a perimeter and looking in the bushes for another gunman. One group spotted Drega on the corner of Bridge and Main Street as he drove north in the police cruiser.

When Drega pulled up to the *Sentinel*, Karen and Beno Lamontagne, proprietors of Lazerworks across the street, were talking to a customer when the cruiser pulled up. They heard the shots and saw Dennis struggling with Drega. Beno ran towards them, shouting for Drega to stop, then screamed back at Karen, "He's shooting Dennis!" Karen says, "I screamed at Beno and went to drag him back inside."

Beno and Karen, along with a woman who had been walking along the street, went back inside as Drega walked toward them and got into the cruiser. "He sat there for a while, then slowly pulled down the street," said Karen. "I ran out the door toward Dennis and then saw Drega slowly make a U-turn and come back." Everyone ran back inside the store, as they watched Drega hesitate in front of the Baptist church, then slowly pull out to stop at the corner of Main Street, before finally turning south.

Karen, an RN, ran to where Dennis had fallen. "After Dennis fell, Drega had walked back to the corner and put more bullets into Vickie which were unnecessary and then walked back to Dennis and put more into him, before he walked away."

Karen, who found Susan Zizza kneeling next to Dennis, saw that he was breathing and had a strong pulse. "I dug out the ground around his nose to make it easier for him to breathe and got paper towels to press around the wound in his back. Susan held the towel while I went to Vickie." Vickie's pulse was fluttering out and Karen knew she was dying. She left Yvette Collins, Pastor Charles Collins' wife, who had joined her, with Vickie and returned to Dennis, who she felt had the best chance of survival. "It was a horrible decision to make." Pastor Collins was with Susan, them EMTs began converging on the area and began working on Dennis. Jeannette, Vivien, and Leith were standing by when the EMTs began arriving. "I could see Susan lying on the ground with her head next to Dennis and thought I heard her saying, 'Dennis, don't leave us.' The sight almost tore my heart out."

"At first," said Karen, "Dennis was responding to [Susan's] voice, but then he began to fade away." Although his heart was strong, his lungs were quickly filling up with fluid. He was pronounced dead on arrival at the Upper Connecticut Valley Hospital.

Drega traveled to the Columbia residence of former selectman Kenneth Parkhurst. Kenneth was not home when Drega kicked in the door of his home. Drega searched the home thoroughly before leaving, then he proceeded south again to his residence a few miles away. When Drega arrived home he shaved, then poured diesel fuel throughout his home and set it on fire. He slightly torched the front door of his barn before leaving the property with the cruiser loaded with ammunition.

The Colebrook Fire Department was dispatched to Drega's house from the scene at LaPerle's IGA. They went in cautiously and started to fight the intense fire. Realizing immediately that the fire was suspicious, they backed away and controlled the burn. They regrouped and decided to stay away from the barn. The fire marshall was called in.

Drega traveled south to Stratford, where he was intercepted by Conservation Officer Wayne Saunders near the Stratford Fire Station. Crossing the bridge into Vermont, Drega turned south on Route 102. Passing under the railroad bridge he pulled abruptly to the side of the road and climbed the embankment. He took a position on the railroad bed above just as Officer Saunders approached the area in his department's Chevy Blazer. Drega opened fire at Officer Saunders through the windshield. His badge deflected a shot intended for his heart and probably saved his life. A second bullet struck him in the shoulder. (He was later airlifted by DART helicopter to the Dartmouth–Hitchcock Medical Center.)

Drega continued south on Route 102. He abandoned the cruiser in a small corn-filled valley near Brunswick Springs on a secluded logging road. He turned the cruiser, parked it facing west, and turned the volume of the cruiser's radio as high as it would go. Removing his shirt, he laid it over the steering wheel with the arms draped over the dash. Police suspect that he wanted them to think that he had committed suicide.

He left the car armed with about 400 rounds of ammunition for his AR-15. He also carried the 9 mm pistol, with a laser-guided scope, loaded with 11 rounds. Unaware that he had been discovered, he then backtracked about 200 feet down the road and hiked up a 20-foot steep embankment to lie in wait behind a large pine tree.

Brunswick Constable Dean Hook and his son, Daniel, spotted Scott's cruiser with the telltale SP608 license plates while out walking in the area. They immediately crept back to the road and alerted troopers in position on Dennis Pond Road, the command post where roughly half of the 60 to 80 officers were stationed. The team was under the command of Lieutenant Leo "Chuck" Jellison.

A small group of officers moved in, including Vermont Trooper Jeff Caulder, New Hampshire Trooper Robert Haase, and Border Patrol Agent John Pfeifer. Everything was working according to Drega's apparent plan until one of the German shepherd dogs with the initial search party spotted him and alerted the six officers.

As they dove for cover, Drega fired off six rounds from the AR-15. Three of the shots found their mark, striking Trooper Caulder in the leg and Border Patrol Agent Pfeifer in the chest. Trooper Haase was hit in the foot by shrapnel.

The group returned the fire as they assisted Trooper Caulder from the scene, then Agent Pfeifer, who was critically injured. Meanwhile, Drega was filling the air with a steady volley of rounds.

Lieutenant Jellison dispatched Detective Corporal Charles West to the area along with Vermont State Police Detective Sergeant Robert van Damm, Essex County Sheriff Amos Colby, and Border Patrol Agent Stephen Brooks. The police helicopter swooped in low to observe Drega from a safe distance.

In the firefight that followed Drega was struck by four bullets: one slug to the chest hit the Kevlar flack jacket that he had removed from Scott's cruiser and two .40-caliber slugs struck him in the back and also became imbedded in the vest. The fatal bullet, caliber unknown, entered Drega's mouth, broke his jaw, and severed an artery in his neck before exiting. In his autopsy it was discovered that he also had a broken rib and a bruised lung. More than 200 spent rounds were found near his body.

All the officers injured in the firefight have since been released from the hospital with the exception of Border Patrol Agent John Pfeifer, who is listed in satisfactory condition.

Source: Reprinted with permission of the *News and Sentinel,* Colebrook, NH.

Drega had more than 600 pounds of ammonium nitrite in three outbuildings on his property. He also had constructed sophisticated booby traps located on his property close to his home. Ammonium nitrate mixed with diesel fuel was the explosive used in the Oklahoma City bombing case of Timothy McVeigh as well as the World Trade Center bombing case. On the same day, Drega had bought 61 gallons of diesel fuel. Some of the fuel was used to burn down his home as the mass murder case was developing.

Drega had a long-standing feud with local government leaders over issues surrounding zoning issues. If this were the precipitating stimulus in this case, it will never be verified. What was known was that before this escapade of murder, the man was judged by many as being strange and peculiar. Others were more concerned about the community's safety and thought him to be dangerous. This certainly turned out to be the case.

The first murder was committed at one place, the former workplace of McCree. The second case of mass murder was committed at two separate sites. If one insists upon restricting the murderous sites to one in the definition of mass murder, the Colebrook murder case is not a mass murder incident. In the Drega case, the killer went from one site, where he murdered two people, to another location a few blocks away, where he murdered again. From the perspective of this book, this must be considered a single act of mass murder, despite the slightly varying times and locations.

A definition of mass murder should include the following elements (Holmes and Holmes, 1995 p. 53):

- The number of victims
- The location of the murders
- The time of the killings
- The possibility of distance between the murders

The components listed above become vitally important when differentiating between mass murder and serial murder. Why is this important? "The determination of the type of homicide holds the key to understanding the character of the person who would commit such an act and enables law enforcement to put into motion the procedures and protocol called for in such a situation" (ibid.).

DIFFERENCES BETWEEN MASS AND SERIAL MURDER

There are fundamental differences between mass murderers and serial murderers. First, the mass killer often dies at the scene of the crime or only a short distance away. Typically, mass killers either commit suicide or place themselves in a situation such that they "force" the police to kill them—perhaps another form of suicide, a "suicide by proxy." McCree committed suicide at the place where he killed five former fellow workers. Drega was involved in a shootout with law enforcement officers. Four bullets struck him. Around his body were found 200 spent rounds. Another mass killer, Paul Ely, Jr., killed his two small children and a police officer and then killed himself. In San Ysidro, California, James Oliver Huberty shot 40 people; 21 died. He was killed by a police sharpshooter who was stationed across the street. In rare cases the mass killer is captured unharmed or simply surrenders to the police. In 1995, Michael Vernon robbed a shoe store in New York City and killed five people. He was wounded and captured as he left the store. Also in 1995, James Floyd Davis surrendered to the police in Asheville, North Carolina, after he had killed three fellow workers. Barry Loukaitis, age 14, went into his high school classroom and killed his teacher, Leona Caires, and classmates Arnold Fritz and Emilio Vela, both age 14. He surrendered to the police (*Courier-Journal*, Louisville, KY, September 25, 1997, p. A2). Needless to say, when one deals with human beings there are no axioms of total truth and reliability, simply probabilities. In serial murder, the serial killer takes great pains to avoid detection (Egger, 1997; Hickey, 1997; Holmes and Holmes, 1998a). Serial murder is not a single episode of violence. It is a series of murders, murders that contain a gain that is not usually spent after administering pain and suffering for a real or alleged mistreatment.

Another difference between mass and serial murderers is the standard that serial killers do not wish to stop killing, whereas the mass killer does appear to take the position that this is a final act of defiance, for whatever reason.

The case of Patrick Purdy illustrates this act of final defiance. Purdy, an obviously troubled young man of 24, dressed himself early one morning in Army fatigues and drove his station wagon to the local elementary school in Stockton, California. He carried a Chinese-made AK-47 to the schoolyard, where he had played as a youth, and opened fire on 450 children. Five children died and 30 others were wounded, along with a teacher. After the shooting stopped, Purdy took a pistol from his jacket and shot himself in the head. He died at the scene. ("Slaughter in a schoolyard," *Time*, January 30, 1989, p. 29).

The murdered children were all of Southeast Asian descent. Purdy had complained about immigrants who entered the United States and contributed to the unemployment rate, inflation, and many other social and economic problems. Focusing his rage against the children made no sense to the citizens of this community or the citizens of the nation. Depressed, full of rage, unable to accomplish anything meaningful in his life, he committed one final, horrible act and then took his own life, as do many mass killers.

This statement about mass killers appears to be true with the possible exception of the set-and-run or revenge mass killer, who we deal with in Chapter 8. Also, very few serial killers, for example, commit suicide or simply stop. One exception who comes to mind immediately is Edmund Kemper. Kemper killed his mother, his mother's best friend, and six college coeds. After driving from California to Colorado, Kemper had an attack of conscience. He called the Santa Cruz Police Department and turned himself in to authorities, saying that "the killings had to stop" (Cheney, 1977; Home Box Office, 1984). Kemper was different from mass killers as well as many other serial killers including Bundy, Gacy, Lucas, and Toole. The mass murderer has no intent to kill again and usually has no intent to turn himself or herself in to the law enforcement community. He or she will often be willing to die at the scene.

Community reaction to a mass murder incident is also different from the reaction to a serial murder case. For instance, in a mass murder case, the immediate community, as well as the nation at large, is affected immediately. The media, both local and national news stations, are quick to arrive at the scene. The top national news reporters and local anchors are at the scene gathering information as they speak. A state of near panic is prevalent throughout the community, but this sense of personal vulnerability is short-lived and leaves almost as soon as it arrives. Slowly, but certainly, the atmosphere of the social climate returns and "normalcy" returns to the city, town, or village. This is not true in a serial murder case. This sense of dread is often permanent and persistent once a community has been affected by a serial killer. The name of the killer and the names of the victims become a part of local history. There is no end of the fear and dread in a serial murder case until the serial killer is apprehended or is determined dead. Witness the case of the Green River Killer in Seattle, Washington. Killing in the early 1980s, this serial murderer has not been caught. There is still a sense of fear and dread because this is still an "open" case (Hickey, 1997; Smith and Guillen, 1990). Thus dread of this unresolved serial murder case remains.

With a mass killer, it is often reported (many times after the fact) that the murderer exhibited certain personality traits that should have alerted those around him that he was a potential mass killer (Kelleher, 1997; Levin and Fox, 1985). In the case of Joseph Wesbecker, a killer we speak of in Chapter 6, several fellow employees of Wesbecker knew that someday he would probably come back to the plant where he had been granted a mental disability and kill some people. Even when the shots were being fired by this disgruntled employee, one worker said to another in the cafeteria, "I bet that's crazy Joe Wesbecker coming back to kill us all" (Holmes and Holmes, 1992, p. 55). Another employee told the police later that Wesbecker had told him that he planned on flying in a model plane armed with a bomb, exploding it once it got inside the plant (ibid.)!

Some serial and mass killers are psychotic (Holmes and DeBurger, 1985, 1988; Holmes and Holmes, 1994, 1998a): They see visions and hear voices. With mass killers, however, such examples are relatively few. One example is Priscilla Ford, who heard the voice of God telling her to kill, then drove to downtown Reno, Nevada, where she ran over a group of pedestrians along a sidewalk. Another example is Brad Bishop, a government worker living in Maryland. He told his psychiatrist that he heard a voice inside him commanding him to kill. In 1985, Sylvia Seegrist went into a local shopping mall and opened fire with an automatic rifle, killing three and wounding seven innocent shoppers. Her mother noted that she had been acting strangely prior to the killings.

Our research suggests that the psychotic mass killer is rare. Most have the mental "health" to plan and carry out the killings, depending on a multitude of factors and motivations that often have little to do with psychosis. However, we have included in this book a separate category, psychotic mass killers. There appear to be more "visionary" (psychotic) serial killers who pose a real and present danger to society than psychotic mass killers.

Serial killers often blend well into society. Ted Bundy was a law student and an assistant director of the Seattle Crime Commission (Michaud and Aynesworth, 1983). Jerry Brudos was a steady worker at an electronics company (Stack, 1983). Douglas Clark was an engineer at a factory (personal interview, June 13, 1993). Beoria Simmons was a social worker (personal interview, Lt. George Barrett, Louisville Police Department, November 19, 1998). All blended in well, and people were surprised when each of these serial killers was arrested and charged with multiple murders. The secret life of a serial killer is known only to the victims; the public life of a serial killer is prosocial and nonthreatening. A mass killer has front-stage behavior that sends behavioral signs that he or she is a threat to some people, especially those who are intended victims. "It is the early detection of the front stage behavior of the mass killer that may alert to the catastrophic back stage behavior which may follow" (Holmes and DeBurger, 1985).

THEORY AND CLASSIFICATION OF MASS MURDER

One method of determining the problem of mass murder is to develop a typology of mass killers. Social and behavioral scientists are adept at developing such typologies in an attempt to better understand the dynamics of behavior as well as contributing factors in the development of the mass murderer. "Such constructs are often based upon behavioral dynamics, motivation, victim characteristics and selection methodologies, loci of motivations and anticipated rewards" (Holmes and DeBurger, 1985). This method was used by Holmes and DeBurger (1988) in their work on serial murder. This typology of serial murderers is widely cited as an instrument of analysis and discussion.

Behavioral Background

The exact etiology of the personality of the mass killer is unknown. As true as it is that the basic personalities of the serial killer and the mass murderer are different, it is also true that the basic causes of the mass killer are also different. It is perhaps a unique combination of biological heredity, social environment (including family interactions, etc.), and specific psychology of the person who will later in life become a mass murderer. These elements alone and in combination, account for the personality of each of us; they also account for the formation of the personality of the mass killer.

Certainly, no single factor accounts for the personality of the mass killer. The total personality of the mass killer cannot easily be explained by examining any one experience or factor in the life of such a murderer. Additionally, there is no evidence indicating that a single biological factor makes a mass killer. Despite the cases of Charles Whitman, Richard Speck, and others suggesting that a biological anomaly resulted in the formation of a mass killer, it has not been proven substantially that this causes someone to become a killer, either serial or mass (Hickey, 1997; Holmes and Holmes, 1994; Sears, 1991). Also, the claims of Norris and

Birnes (1988) that a blow to the head causes someone to become a killer is suspect, especially since there is no documentation behind his work. The basic causes of crime and delinquency that have been popular for the last 40 years—poverty, female-headed families, and other—do not explain mass murder any more than they explain simple criminal or delinquent behavior. If these factors did provide an exact script for mass predation, all people who suffered these experiences would be mass killers. This is simply not the case. Holmes and DeBurger report: bad neighborhoods, economic stress, family stability, and violence in the culture do not directly produce serial murderers. Out of a cohort that experiences the worst possible combinations of social stresses, relatively few will engage in outright criminal behavior and fewer still will engage in outright criminal behavior and fewer still will become homicidal…" (1988, p. 48).

Motivation

Motivation is another element used to categorize mass killers (Holmes, 1994). The motivation to kill a number of unrelated and unknown victims in one act of mass predation is complex and certainly not easily understood, or, perhaps, ever understandable. A partial answer may lie in the location of the motivation within or extrinsic to the personality.

For example, there may be something deep within the personality of a mass killer that impels him or her to commit an act of mass murder. Witness the case of Priscilla Ford. Receiving a vision from God, she ran over pedestrians in her automobile. Mass killers, along with serial killers, often tell of an "entity" that commands that they kill.

With James Huberty the motivation to kill rested within Huberty himself. For a myriad of reasons ranging perhaps from occupational and social class frustration to other stresses, he killed—not because someone commanded him to, but because he believed that society was operating against him, and he was reacting to the injustices he perceived in society (Holmes and DeBurger, 1985, p. 56.)

More likely, the motivation to kill comes from outside the personality (Holmes and Holmes, 1994). It is not a personality defect, a psychotic episode, or a series of such episodes that make the person kill a group of people. Consider the case of the mass murder scene at the home of Sharon Tate. The members of the Charlie Manson "family" killed five people that dreadful night. The motivation to kill rested outside their personalities—Charlie Manson was the source of their motivation (Bugliosi and Gentry, 1976). The members of his family wanted to please him. The way to please him was to follow orders and kill those unfortunate victims who just happened to be on the grounds and in the house at that particular time.

Anticipated Gain

What is the reason for an act of mass murder, and what does the murderer hope to gain from this act of homicide? There are two types of anticipated gain: (1) *psychological* and (2) *material*, that is, *expressive* or *instrumental*. The psychological gain from the act of mass murder rests not with money, wealth, business interest, or insurance claims. It rests more with the perceived realization that people may now stand up and take notice of troubling issues that are important to the mass killer. Nonetheless, the examination of anticipated gain is important in any consideration of a mass killer.

Spatial Mobility

In examining many cases of mass murder, the killer is found predominately to be geographically stable. Most live in the area in which they work and kill in the same area; they are not nomadic in their killings. They often kill in a place where they work, recreate, or in some cases where their spouse or significant other is employed. Spatial mobility does not normally play an integral role, with the exception of the mass killer who is hired to set fire to a building for the owner to recapture a financial loss, or a member of a terrorist group, to select a target of innocents (e.g., Timothy McVeigh).

Victim Characteristics

Victim traits or characteristics do not play an integral element in the mass murder process. Usually, the victims are unknown to the mass killer; the family annihilator is the exception. The victim may simply be in the wrong place at the wrong time. In Luby's restaurant in Killeen, Texas, customers were simply having lunch when a mass killer drove his pickup truck through the front window. They had no relationship with George Hennard. Some may have known him only as another resident of this small Texas town—nothing more. The customers at the McDonald's restaurant in San Ysidro, California, had no relation to Huberty. The same can be said of the purchasers of Tylenol in the Chicago episode; they were merely buying a product at varied and unrelated stores.

In examining the victim relationships and traits, it is readily apparent that in dealing with most mass murderers, there is no prior personal relationship between the killer and the victims. In the case of the mass killer who returns to his place of employment and kills fellow workers and supervisors, there is a personal relationship, although small, between the two. In the case of the killer who kills his family, the relationship is personal.

The traits of the victims of a mass killer are not important. Hair color or style, body build, or other physical attributes are inconsequential. The fetishisms that are present with a serial killer are not present with the mass killer. There is no need for them since mass killers usually do not kill for the same reasons as those of the serial murderer. Few, if any, are committed for a sexual motivation, which is a common motivation for the serial killer (Egger, 1997; Hickey, 1997; Holmes and Holmes, 1998).

Usually, no stalking behavior is involved with a mass killer. The victims are simply in the wrong place at the wrong time. Whether at work or at leisure, they usually share only space and time with the mass killer—again with the exception of a person who kills family members.

TYPOLOGY OF MASS MURDERERS

Several major types of mass killers were found in a review of the literature: the pseudocommando, the disciple, the family annihilator, the religious/ideological killer, the disgruntled citizen, the disgruntled employee, the set-and-run killer, and the psychotic mass killer (Dietz, 1986; Holmes and Holmes, 1994). The elements of motivation, anticipated gain, victim selectivity, victim relationship, spatial mobility, and victim traits will be examined as they apply to each type of mass killer. We need to mention here the groundbreaking work of Park Dietz in his original typology of mass killers, which we relied on heavily in this work. The family annihilator, the disgruntled type, the set-and-run type, and the pseudocommando all result from the work of Dietz; the others are ours. We have included Dietz's work as a sign of our appreciation of his work. We thank him.

It is not our intention in this chapter to explore the various types of mass killers. We consider many of the individual types later in the book. Our purpose here is to introduce the typology. In subsequent chapters we develop the typology more fully, when exploring various types in case study form.

Here we speak briefly of several types that have been developed.

The first mass killer is the *disciple killer*. This mass killer kills because of the relationship with someone who dictates the murder. In Chapter 4 the relationship between the charismatic leader and the disciple killer is explored and assumptions made about the influence the leader has on the activities and behavior of the killer. The classic case of the Charles Manson family is discussed.

The next mass killer is the *family annihilator*. This killer murders those he knows: family members, relatives, common-law relatives, and so on. This killer operates from an intrinsic motivation, and his anticipated gain is expressive or psychological. Ronald Gene Simmons, a retired Air Force sergeant, is such an example. So is John List, a family annihilator we have chosen to illustrate as an example of this type of mass killer.

The next mass murderer is the *disgruntled employee*. This type of mass killer typically returns to a former place of employment and kills those who are "responsible" for his problems. Often, this type of killer has severe emotional and psychiatric problems and is on medication for these mental and physical conditions. Unfortunately, he often kills innocent bystanders, sometimes those who have worked side by side with him. Joseph Wesbecker is such an example.

The next type of mass killer is the *ideological mass murderer*. This killer kills those whom he knows, usually members of his own group or cult and himself. In this book, Heaven's Gate and Jim Jones are discussed.

The next type of mass killer is the *set-and-run mass killer*. This type of murderer is usually away from the scene of the crime by the time the victims are killed. Some may question why we placed the Timothy McVeigh Oklahoma City bombing case in this chapter rather than in the ideological mass murder chapter. This type of killer arranges for some type of explosive or other device to be set and then separates himself from the site. This was certainly true in the case of McVeigh. The victim relationship is also different. A mass killer of the ideological ilk murders members of his own group or cult. With a set-and-run killer, the victims are strangers. Such was the case of McVeigh, who killed 168 people, 20 of them children. We have also included the unresolved mass murder Tylenol case.

The *disgruntled citizen* is similar to the disgruntled employee. However, his victims are innocent bystanders who share no space or relationship with the killer. They just happen to be in the same space at the time of the murderous incident. George "Jo Jo" Hennard is the example we have chosen for this type of killer.

The *psychotic mass murderer* is yet another type of mass killer. This perpetrator is out of touch with reality. The killer may hear voices or see visions that command that he or she kill innocent strangers. Some examples of this type of mass killer have already been mentioned, and in Chapter 10 we discuss the special problems and concerns of this mass killer.

CONCLUSION

In the short time since we began writing this book, there have been many other cases of mass murder. Michael Carneal is such an example. Additionally, there is no reason to expect that the number of mass murder incidents will stop. There will always be mass murderers as well as serial murder cases and other forms of homicide.

To deal with the social problem of mass murder, the initial stage is to attempt to develop an understanding of the nature of mass murder. Examining various types of mass killers is perhaps one step in the development of an understanding of the mass murderer's personality. This typology provides a mechanism for examining the anticipated gains, locus of motivation, victim information, and murderer mobility of each type of mass murderer.

The examination of such traits will serve as a basis for an examination of each type of mass killer. The format in the chapters is similar. This is intentional; it is not, however, intended to be simply repetitive. By examining each type in a similar fashion, the reader will be able to distinguish the factors that separate one type of mass killer from others.

Discussion Questions

1. What is the nationally and generally recognized definition of a serial killer? How does this definition differ with regard to mass murderers?

2. In your opinion, in regard to the definition of a mass murderer, what difference does it make if a victim is either injured or killed?

3. What national implications can the variety of definitions associated with mass or spree killers have on the government's or a local agency's ability to enforce either legislation or treatment of potential mass murderers?

4. Similarly, what effect may the confusing number of definitions regarding the number of kills or injuries have on the public's conception of how large a social problem mass murder is in contemporary U.S. society?

5. In differentiating between mass and serial murderers, why do you think that mass murderers appear to take the position that the homicidal event will be their last living act? What does this say about the mass or spree killer?

6. Why do you think that serial murderers, as opposed to mass murderers, often hear voices or see demons compelling them to commit homicidal events? How does this affect detection or early warning systems throughout a community that a person needs help?

7. List and describe the seven types of mass murderers described in this chapter. How are they similar, and how are they different?

CHAPTER 4

The Disciple Mass Killer

Luke Woodham apologized to the family of his victims in an exclusive interview with ABC News on January 14, 1998. He said in that interview that he felt that he was an outcast in society, felt alone and harrassed. He added that he was influenced by a group of fellow students in his small Mississippi town and plotted to take over the town. Despite this apology and admission, in court, Woodham still pleaded innocent to the charges of killing his mother and two students in his high school.

In Middlebury, Vermont, a gunman identified as Richard Stevens shot three people near a college campus in this small New England town on April 17, 1996. His body was found in an apartment close to the college campus. He had killed himself. Some believed that he had dabbled in the occult.

INTRODUCTION

In starting this chapter we establish a format that will be followed in subsequent chapters. First we introduce the type of mass killer we will be examining. Next, we examine the various traits of that mass killer. For example, in this chapter we examine the various traits of the disciple mass killer. After examining the various traits of the mass killer, we further illustrate the type of killer with a case history.

In discussing each type of mass killer, we examine the typology that we established in Chapter 3 in the section "Theory and Classification of Mass Murder." In this way, each will be compared to the other types; thus a constant frame of reference can be maintained. Distinctions are made considering the manner in which they are motivated, the victim selection process, spatial mobility, and various victim traits. Each type will emerge from this examination with a distinct profile not only as to the manner in which they kill but also in their selection of victims.

The disciple mass murderer kills because of the relationship that exists between the killer and the leader of a group to which the killer belongs. The "reason to be" will vary from one group to another. The reason for the existence of the group may be political (and in the Jonestown massacre, partially religious), revolutionary (the Charles Manson family), or another reason. The guiding force goes beyond the philosophy of the group to the leadership. Leadership is usually predicated on their being a charming and charismatic leader who lends not only a philosophy but also a plan for action to accomplish the group's goal. The plan for action and the goals of the group are carefully stated by the leader and his or her inner circle of confidantes. The message is sometimes delivered to the followers as coming from God, sent through the leader, who may be considered a prophet who shares a special relationship with God. It is through this relationship that the plans, goals, and objectives gain acceptance by those in the fold. If the message comes directly from the leader, the special personality traits of the leader engender a willingness to accept the plans, goals, and objectives. A charismatic leader is able to convince the followers to surrender their individuality for the good of the group. Often, the members will give up not only their own wants and desires but also their financial holdings. This was evident in the Manson family, the Branch Davidians, and the disciples of David Koresch.

There are many cases of disciple mass killers, but we have chosen to illustrate the case of the disciple mass killer by the Manson family. This case is also perhaps the best known of murder by those who follow a leader. The followers of Charles Manson included Susan Atkins, Sandra Good, Charles Watson, Patricia Krenwinkel, Leslie Van Houten, and Linda Kasabian.

Traits of Mass Murderers.

Using the same format for each type, we will be able to distinguish among them. In all cases we examine the following elements:

- Motivation
- Anticipated gain
- Victim selectivity
- Victim relationship
- Spatial mobility
- Victim traits

We investigate the same traits, in the same order, to determine the differences. Some share traits. For example, the disciple killer and the set-and-run killer all select strangers as victims. This trait is different from that of the family annihilator, for example, who kills family members (sometimes extended family members), and that of the disgruntled citizen, who often kills people in his or her place of employment or people in the neighborhood. In other words, the latter two types of mass killers may not kill complete strangers; for example, the disgruntled citizen killer has not had the opportunity to become personally acquainted with all the victims. This circumstance is addressed in chapter 9.

TRAITS OF THE DISCIPLE MASS KILLER

Let us now turn to a discussion of the disciple mass murderer and the traits that distinguish this killer from other types of mass murderers (See Table 4.1).

Motivation. ***The motivation is extrinsic to the personality of the killer.*** With a mass killer of the disciple type, the desire to kill a number of persons arises not from within the mind of the killer but from the relationship between the killer and the leader of the assembly. The relationship that exists between these two actors contributes to the victimization at the killing scene.

On the one hand, the leader of the group is commanding the murder of a certain group of people. On the other hand, the disciple or follower is willing to follow an order to kill with such dedication and zeal that there is never a moment of hesitation or refusal. It is what the leader wishes, and that is all that truly matters. The motivation to kill arises not because of some dark need inside the mind of the killer but from the need for the killer to feel accepted and part of the inner membership of the group. One could make an argument that the killer indeed is motivated to kill from a point somewhere inside the person's mind. This is certainly true but only to a small degree. The larger part of the motivation rests outside the mind. As difficult as it may be to understand why one would be willing

---

TABLE 4.1   Traits of the Disciple Mass Killer

Motivation
   Intrinsic
   Extrinsic
	The motivation is extrinsic to the mind of the killer.

Anticipated gain
   Expressive
   Instrumental
	The gain is expressive, or psychological, to the killer.

Victim selectivity
   Random
   Nonrandom
	Victims are usually selected on a random basis; the leader determines who will be victims.

Victim relationship
   Affiliative
   Strangers
	The victims are typically strangers to the killer.

Spatial mobility
   Stable
   Transient
	The killer is geographically transient and will follow the movements of the leader.

Victim traits
   Specific
   Nonspecific
	The traits are nonspecific because the victims are unimportant to the killer.

to murder because someone else desires it to be done, we are all familiar with these kinds of cases. The holocaust illustrates this well. Soldiers killed innocent men, women, and children because they were instructed to do so. There was a plan, objectives, and rationalizations to kill. Personal responsibility was absent. The leader, Hitler, offered a plan to those people who were willing to accept it to belong to the chosen group.

The disciple killer is only doing what is necessary to gain acceptance. The acceptance is internal. The commandment by the leader to kill is a statement extrinsic to the mind of the killer; the motivation rests outside the mind. This acceptance is the reason that the mass killer carries out the command to murder a number of people. If the motivation to kill were intrinsic to the mind of the killer, there would be an inner force demanding the fatal dispatchment of a group of people. The victims would be chosen by the killer. But in this instance, it rests within the mind of the leader. The disciple murders because he or she wishes or requires the acceptance of the leader. Leslie Van Houten killed because of the relationship that she had with Charlie Manson; the same can be said of the other followers of the Manson family (Sanders, 1971).

Anticipated Gain.   ***The anticipated gain is expressive, not material.*** What does this mass killer wish to gain from the acts of mass fatal predation? This killer, along with other murderers, wishes something to be realized from the acts of murder. With some killers, the gain is material. A professional hit man, a killer for the mob, for example, kills for monetary or instrumental gain. Richard Kuklinski, a serial killer, killed by his own admission scores of people, sometimes for money. He stated that he killed in a variety of ways, with handguns, shotguns, or poisons. The reasons for the killings were varied. In some cases the victim owed him money, and sometimes he was paid to kill by organized crime members (Bruno, 1993).

The disciple killer, however, wishes a gain that is expressive or psychological. What this killer wishes is the acceptance of the leader. The mass murderer believes that killing a predetermined group will bring the killer's case for acceptance into a positive perspective and will gain his or her personal acceptance by the leader. There is no money to be exchanged. There is no one to pay the killer in the same way that was instrumental in the Kuklinski case. The acceptance is psychological for the killer.

Victim Selectivity.   ***The victims are selected on a random basis.*** Because of the nature of the mass murder the disciple killer perpetrates, the traits or characteristics of the victims are unimportant. Thus the victims need not have personal traits that are attractive to the mass killer. The motivation to kill is involved in the relationship with the charismatic leader of the group. The people chosen to be killed are typically unknown to the disciple killer. The victims are known or selected to reinforce a philosophical, dogmatic, or other position by the disciple. So the point here is that the victims are clearly the choice of the leader. Although more than 900 people were killed in Jonestown, Jim Jones did not kill all of them himself. He had fanatical helpers to help prepare the potion that poisoned his followers.

Finally, one of the followers shot him in the head and then killed himself. What was to be gained from the killings of such a large number of followers? The gain was psychological: to be a part of the circle of believers, to escape the tyranny of government interference, and to gain everlasting salvation.

In summary:

- The disciple killer murders those who are chosen by the leader of the group.
- The names, traits, and characteristics of the victims are unimportant to the killer(s).
- The victims are often unknown to the killer(s).
- The murders are utilitarian, not sexual.
- The victims may be known to the leader.
- The murders may only be a test of the fidelity of the killer(s) to the leader.
- The victims themselves have little importance to the disciple mass killer.

Victim Relationship. ***The victims are typically strangers to the disciple killer.*** The victims are usually not related to the disciple mass killer. Unlike some other types of mass murderers, the victims are usually selected randomly, as stated above, and are strangers to the killer. Most often, there is no victim-precipitated relationship with the disciple killer. The victims play no or a minimal role in their own victimization. They are strangers to the killer and are selected only because they are targeted for some reason by the leader of the group itself. Charlie Manson selected the victims at Sharon Tate's home. The identities of the victims were unknown to the members of the Manson group. Even Steven Parent, leaving the premises in his car, was killed by Manson's followers. The next night, Manson demanded again another murder, and the members followed Charlie to the second home. Charlie left before the murders began but after he gave the orders to kill (Bugliosi and Gentry, 1976; Sanders, 1971).

There are no innocent victims of a disciple killer. The victims are viewed more as objects (Holmes and Holmes, 1994). The "objects" must be eliminated so that the group will remain viable. In the final analysis, people are killed simply because they are selected by the leader.

Spatial Mobility. ***The killer tends to be geographically transient.*** The members of a cult or group that follows a charismatic leader often appear to be searching for a relationship. They may travel from one location to another in their search. This was certainly true of the members of the Charles Manson family. Not only may they come from sometimes far-flung areas to be around their leader, they are also willing to follow their leader to wherever the leader wishes to go in a personal search for fulfillment.

It may be that younger potential members of this type of group will be more inclined to be geographically stable, if only because of financial constraints or

Case Study

The Charles Manson Family

No one case of mass murder captured America's attention so much as the case of Charles Manson and his family in the 1960s (see Table 4.2). Born in 1934 to a prostitute, Charles Manson accumulated an extensive record as a juvenile. As a young adult he was arrested several times for stealing cars, theft, and pimping. He spent a good portion of his youth behind bars in juvenile institutions. He was later sentenced to a prison term and was released at the time the free love movement of the 1960s was in full bloom. He married, quickly divorced, and moved to California. There he surrounded himself with young people who looked upon him as a father figure and a savior. He implied to his followers that he was a reincarnation of Jesus Christ, describing himself as the "Son of Man."

Settling in a dilapidated former movie ranch with his followers, Charlie initiated his group into his dogma. Obsessed with the Beatles, he believed that their songs were written especially for him, particularly "Helter Skelter." The words of the song convinced him that the end of the world was coming and that he and his followers were the only ones who would survive the end of the world. To do that he would go into the desert where the bombs could not reach and a race war would ensue. Following that, the family would rule the country. To start the battle between the races, Manson ordered the killings.

Indeed, Manson is in prison for murders that occurred on two separate occasions. But Manson himself may have been involved in a series of murders. He boasted to a prosecutor, Vincent Bugliosi, that he has himself killed 35 people, a boast that Bugliosi believes may be underestimated.

On August 9, 1969, Manson family members Tex Watson, Patricia Krenwinkel, Susan Atkins, and Linda Kasabian broke into the home of Roman Polanski and Sharon Tate. Polanski was out of the country making a film. At home were Tate, Abigail Folger, Jay Sebring, and Voyteck Frykowski. On the grounds, driving toward the front gate, was 18-year-old Steven Parent. All were brutally murdered. Sharon Tate was tied with a rope around her neck and connected to her friend Jay Sebring, who who had been beaten to death. Frykowski and Folger, the heiress to the family coffee fortune, were found on the grounds outside the home. Charlie's followers had written in blood on the walls "PIG" and "HELTER SKELTER."

Two nights later, Charlie and several family members, including Watson, Atkins, Krenwinkel, Kasabian, Grogan, and Van Houten, went into the home of a grocery chain store tycoon and his wife, Leno and Rosemary LaBianca. The couple was still alive when Charlie left; they died shortly thereafter. Mrs. LaBianca was stabbed repeatedly. Mr. LaBianca was found with a knife and a fork stuck in his chest.

The police investigated this case with great vigor. These two murders shocked the citizens of Los Angeles, and they demanded quick resolution of the crimes. Were they related? Some believed they were, but for similar reasons, the police were reluctant to release their opinion that the murders were probably committed by the same persons.

Susan Atkins, a member of the Manson family, was arrested for a different offense and boasted to another prisoner in her jail cell what she had done. She admitted that she had killed Sharon Tate and had tasted her blood. The cellmate believed her and informed the police of her boasts. The homicide detectives believed the cellmate and arrested Manson, Susan Atkins (already in jail), Patricia Krenwinkel, Charles (Tex) Watson, and Leslie Van Houten. They were all charged with the murders, tried, and convicted. All were sentenced to death. However, the U.S. Supreme Court decided that the death penalty as administered was unconstitutional, so the defendants' sentences were all commuted to life imprisonment.

In the killing of human beings, disciple killers follow the direction of the leader. In this case of the Manson family, the leader was Charles. He instructed the family members to kill people who were unknown to the killers themselves. They were selected by the leader of the group. They shared no affinity with the victims. They were targets that the leader selected and demanded be killed.

TABLE 4.2   Charles Manson Family Members and Manson Acquaintances

Susan Atkins	Involved in the Tate and LaBianca killings. Also known as Sex Sadie, Sharon King, and Donna Kay Powell.
Bobby Beausoleil	Involved in the Gary Hinman Killing; known as Cupid, Casper, and Janson Lee Daniels.
Mary Brunner	The first young woman to join the family. She may have been involved in the Hinman killing. Known as Mother Mary, Mary Manson, Och, and Linda Dee Moser.
James Craig	Pleaded guilty to being an accessory after the fact in two murders.
Lynette Fromme	One of Manson's earliest followers. She assumed leadership after Manson was arrested. Known as Squeaky. She is presently in prison for attempting to assassinate the president of the United States.
Catherine Gillies	Granddaughter of the owner of the Myers ranch, where the family lived for a time. Also known as Cappy, Patti Sue, and Patricia Ann Burke.
Sandra Good	A family member. She was also known as Sandy.
Steven Grogran	Was with the family on the night of the LaBianca killing. He was also allegedly involved in the Hinman killing and in the attempted murder of a prosecution witness in the trial against Manson.
Gary Hinman	Befriended the Manson family and was murdered by them.
Linda Kasabian	She accompanied the family members on the nights of the Tate and LaBianca killings. She became a witness for the prosecution.
Patricia Krenwinkel	Involved in the Tate and LaBianca killings. Known as Katie, Marnie Reeves, and Big Patty.
Leslie Van Houten	Involved in the LaBianca killing. Also known as Lulu, Leslie Owens, Leslie Marie Sankston, and Louella Alexandria.
Charles Watson	Involved in the Tate and LaBianca killings.

Source: Data from Bugliosi and Gentry (1976).

What would be the gain for murdering unknown victims? It is acceptance into the brotherhood and sisterhood of the group. The gain, then, is psychological. This was evident in the case of the two Manson family murder cases described. The killers murdered only because Charles demanded it. They were attempting to please Manson.

Charles Manson and some of his followers have been incarcerated since 1969. As difficult as it may be to accept, some people in our society may believe that Manson is innocent and await his release. Manson himself has appeared before the parole board on several occasions since his incarceration. His statements to the parole board were convoluted and made little sense, perhaps reflecting a deteriorating mental condition: "Our father who art in heaven, hallowed be thy name. That's my daddy too you know." Also: "I believe in the field of honor. And I believe that if someone offends you that you have the right to smack 'em in the mouth, punch 'em out, and dare 'em to come out and fight till—you know, the field of honor is there., That's the way prison is run. Well, I run that." Also: "I am not a Yankee. I'm a rebel boy out of the hills of Kentucky and Tennessee. I keep telling these people from California that, that they don't understand what a Beverly hillbilly is." *(http://members.tripod.com/~helterskelter/Manson*, November 9, 1997).

The parole board has consistently refused him parole. After his last hearing, Manson was moved to the California State Prison at Corcoran. Searching the Internet, we found his address and were encouraged to write the parole board on his behalf by Lynette Fromme, a former member of the family. Obviously, we have not heard the end of the Charles Manson family.

Source: Information for the Manson family was developed from Buglosi and Gentry (1976), Emmons (1986), Levin and Fox (1985), and Sanders (1971).

parental interference. However, when the means to travel becomes available (money, opportunity, etc.), the person may leave and join a group that meets the psychological needs of the member.

Victim Traits.   ***The traits of the victims are nonspecific:*** The traits of all victims of disciple killers are nonspecific. Unlike serial killers, who deliberately seek out victims because they are most often seeking some form of sexual gratification, the mass killer of the disciple form seeks a victim with no specific physical, personal, or occupational traits. It is the instructions of the leader that announce to the mass killer who the intended victims are. The victims usually share no affinity with the killer or killers.

CONCLUSION

The disciple mass killer will continue to kill innocent people. The key to the successful reduction of this type of mass murder is to identify those kinds of groups that are led by a psychological authority figure who demands absolute control and obedience to the commandments of the leadership. The members of the group will adhere to the leader's demands for reasons that only a deep psychological analysis will be able to determine. The personal necessity to belong to a group at any cost is the basic motivation. Some societal and local actions must be developed to confront and satisfy such needs by providing alternatives to membership in a group or gang that is antisocial in character and action.

Discussion Questions

1. What do you believe are the psychological characteristics of disciples in this form of mass murder?

2. What do you believe would be the traits of a person who could lead a group of followers to commit murder?

3. If Charles Manson were free today, do you believe that he could collect followers who would do his bidding? Why or why not?

4. Are you aware of any cults existing today that could involve themselves in some form of mass murder? Describe them for class discussion.

CHAPTER 5

The Family Annihilator*

Leonardo Morita was in dire financial straits. In May 1995, Leonardo set his home afire, killing his wife, three children, and the housekeeper. Morita was inexperienced and died two months later from injuries he received while setting the fire that killed his family.

James Colbert, age 39, was accused of murdering his family in Concord, New Hampshire. His wife was strangled, and his daughters, age 2 years, 1 year, and 10 weeks, were suffocated. One officer of the local police department said that they dissuaded him from committing suicide by jumping off a bridge into the river. Colbert confessed to the murders of his wife and three children.

Kao Xiong had an argument with his wife on the morning of December 4, 1999. Later that afternoon, he fatally shot his five children, ages 2, 3, 4, 5, and 7. His two other children, ages 8 and 11 escaped. The wife had left home earlier in the day. He then killed himself with a 12-gauge shotgun.

INTRODUCTION

What would impel someone to kill his or her own family? This question has perplexed numerous people both within and outside the criminal justice system. There are many examples of such killers (see Table 5.1). John List, one such killer, murdered his entire family and then escaped detection for years. Another killer, Ronald Gene Simmons, killed several members of his own family. The latter was convicted of his crimes and executed; he demanded his own death. Perhaps one of the best known cases of a family annihilator is the case of Captain Jeffrey MacDonald, an Army physician convicted of the murder of his wife and two daughters (McGinnis, 1985; Potter and Bost, 1997). MacDonald is currently in prison for the murder of his family, despite his protestations of innocence.

---

*The work of Park Dietz is utilized herein when dealing with certain types of mass killers: the family annihilator, the set-and-run killer, and the disgruntled killer. We thank him for his groundbreaking work in this area. See also Chapters 6, 8, and 9.

TABLE 5.1 Selected Alleged and Suspected Family Annihilators, 1980–1999

Name	State	Victims
George Avanesian	California	Killed 7 family members
George Banks	Pennsylvania	Killed 9 family members
David Brown	Minnesota	Axed 4 family members
Michael Brunner	Kentucky	Shot his girlfriend and her 2 children
Dora Buenrostro	California	Stabbed her 3 children
Larry Buttz	Iowa	Killed his wife and 2 children
Kim Chandler	Ohio	Shot her 3 children
Mark Clark	Maryland	Bombed his wife and 3 children
James Colbert	New Hampshire	Killed his wife and 3 children
Peter Contos	Massachusetts	Killed his girlfriend and 2 children
Girley Crum	Oregon	Killed a couple, an adult, and 2 children
Errol Dehaney	Connecticut	Shot his wife and 2 children
Lawrence DeLisle	Michigan	Drowned his 4 children
Paul Ely, Jr.	Alabama	Killed his wife and 2 children
Michael Fisher	Maryland	Killed his mother, stepfather, and stepbrother
Bryan Freeman	Pennsylvania	Killed his parents and brother
David Freeman	Pennsylvania	Killed his parents and brother
Martin Garcia	Washington	Killed his niece and 2 stepchildren
Joshua Jenkins	California	Killed 5 family members
Fred Kornahrens	South Carolina	Killed his wife, her father, and 2 sons
John List	New York	Killed his wife, his mother, and 3 children
Daniel Lyman	Washington	Killed his parents, parents-in-law, his wife, and 2 children
Leonardo Morita	California	Burned his wife, 3 sons, and a maid
Michael Perry	Louisiana	Killed 5 family members
James Schnick	Minnesota	Killed 7 family members
Ronald Simmons	Arkansas	Killed 16 family members
Jeffrey Sloan	Missouri	Killed his parents and 2 brothers
Michael Stevens	New York	Killed his girlfriend's mother, sister, and stepfather
David Vitaver	Florida	Killed his wife, son, and daughter
David Whitson	Oregon	Shot his wife and 3 daughters
James Williams	Alabama	Shot 3 family members
Norman Yazzie	Arizona	Shot his 4 children
Kao Xiong	Hawaii	Shot 5 children and then himself

The family annihilator is different from other mass killers, not only in the identification of victims but also in the method of selection, victim traits, spatial mobility, motivation to kill, and anticipated gain. The family annihilator is intent on killing victims he or she knows well, members of his or her own family. What compels the killer to do this is unique to his or her mind; the rewards are also different. Unlike the disciple killer, this killer does not depend on the instructions of others. The disciple killer depends on the instructions or commandments of the leader of the group. It may be a political ideology; it may be a strike against a company or a group that the killer believes has offended him or her. Or it may be extrinsic: He or she may be in the employ of someone to set fire for insurance money. But with the family annihilator, the victims are those he or she knows. It is killing that is demanded on the personal level of the killer, and the victims are selected only because they are the members of the killer's family and there is a perceived need to eradicate the family (see Table 5.2).

TABLE 5.2   Selected Alleged, Suspected, and Convicted Family Annihilator Mass Killers, 1990s

Name	Victims
Michael Stevens	Fearful that his girlfriend was going to end their relationship, he killed her, her parents, and two bystanders with six mail bombs.
David Whitson	Whitson shot and killed his wife and three daughters in Oregon.
Mark Clark	In Maryland, Clark picked up his wife and three children to go shopping in a mall; he detonated a bomb in his car and killed his family.
James Schnick	In Montana, this mass killer killed seven family members, including four of his own children.
George Banks	A prison guard, Banks killed 13 people, including five of his children and four of the women who were their mothers.
Daniel Lyman	In Tacoma, Washington, Lyman killed his parents, his parents-in-law, his wife, and his two children.
Errol Dehaney	In Connecticut, Dehaney, who had a history of domestic violence, killed his wife and two children.
Dora Buenrostro	Buenrostro killed her three children, all under 10 years of age, in San Jacinto, California.
Martin Garcia	In Carson City, Nevada, this construction worker went to his home and shot and killed his niece and two stepchildren.
Joshua Jenkins	A 15-year-old, Jenkins killed his parents, his grandparents, and the next day, his 10-year-old sister in San Diego, California. When he was arrested he had his grandparents' dog with him.
Mark Christeson, Jesse Carter	In Missouri, these two men allegedly killed a mother and her son and daughter.

Family annihilator Ronald Gene Simmons killed members of his own family, then continued his killing outside his immediate family, including cousins. John List stayed within his immediate family. He murdered his family so he could start another life not weighed down by previous family financial obligations. He was deeply in debt, and he believed that the only way to rid himself of financial ruin was to eliminate his family. After that, he would assume a new identity.

There are others who have killed family members and then left, as well as those who have killed their families and then committed suicide. Perhaps not wanting their loved ones to remain in a world where there is such chaos and destruction, the killer wishes to end the lives of his or her family so they will not have to suffer as he or she is suffering. The killer then usually takes his or her own life to join them in a better time to come. This is not the type of killer we deal with in this chapter.

TRAITS OF THE FAMILY ANNIHILATOR

Let us now move into a further discussion of the various traits of the family annihilator. The same traits that were used to analyze the mindset and psychology of the disciple mass killer are used in this chapter and in all subsequent chapters that deal with the various types of mass killers. These traits are presented in Table 5.3 for the family annihilator.

TABLE 5.3 Traits of the Family Annihilator

Motivation
  Intrinsic
  Extrinsic
	The motivation is intrinsic to the mind of the killer.

Anticipated gain
  Expressive
  Instrumental
	An expressive or psychological gain is anticipated by the killer.

Victim selectivity
  Random
  Nonrandom
	Victims are selected on a nonrandom basis; they are family members.

Victim relationship
  Affiliative
  Strangers
	The victims are relations; they are not strangers, but family members.

Spatial mobility
  Stable
  Transient
	The killer is typically a long-term resident of the area.

Victim traits
  Specific
  Nonspecific
	Physical traits are not important to the killer.

Case Study

Ronald Gene Simmons

Ronald Gene Simmons was an angry and sexually disturbed man. On a day in early 1988, he went on a killing spree that resulted in the deaths of 16 innocent victims. Simmons was retired from the U.S. Air Force as a master sergeant. He was known as an angry man who was difficult to get along with. He had several jobs in the period when he lived in Arkansas and was terminated from his unskilled positions because of his belligerence and his inability, or unwillingness, to get along with fellow workers. Warning signs, in retrospect, were put up by Simmons. For example, in addition to his difficulty in getting along with people, Simmons placed a cinder-block fence around his trailer where he lived with his wife and children. He also put up a "No Trespassing" sign warning intruders of the potential danger if they defied his warning.

Simmons was relatively new to Arkansas. After serving in the Navy and Air Force, he lived in New Mexico. There in 1981, Simmons was charged with three counts of incest. He and the family fled to Arkansas, and he was never prosecuted by the authorities in New Mexico. His mental health deteriorated to the point where he was abusive to his wife and children. One daughter, Loretta, age 17, a later victim, wrote a letter to a high school student: "I'd rather be dead than go on like this. My dad hates me, says I'm not good enough, yet he claims I'm conceited" (*Newsweek*, January 11, 1988, p. 16). Further pathology was evident in the alleged charges of sexual abuse directed toward his wife and children.

Simmons, 47, went into the town of Russellville, Arkansas one day early in January 1988. He shot and killed a former co-worker, Kathy Kendrick, who had spurned his sexual advances. He then went to the office of a former employer, J. D., and killed him. He also wounded another man at that company, but luckily this victim survived that attack. Simmons then went to a convenience store, where he wounded two employees. Finally, he attacked an employee at a freight company. He was coerced out of the business and was taken into custody.

As he was interviewed by the police, he was asked if they could contact someone in his family to tell about the shooting and subsequent arrest. Not receiving an adequate reply, the officers went to the trailer. There they discovered the bodies of four adults and one child. The next day, they uncovered seven corpses in a shallow grave. Shortly after, the authorities found two more bodies in a nearby abandoned car.

Simmons admitted his guilt in the murder of 16 people. As a family annihilator, Simmons fits the profile traits well. Motivation, anticipated gain, victim selectivity, victim relationship, spatial mobility, and victim traits are all evident in his selection of victim, with the exception of the two victims that started the killing, a former co-worker and a woman who he thought he could seduce.

Motivation. ***The motivation is intrinsic to the personality of the killer.*** When one chooses to murder members of one's own family, there is some motivation that will accompany the decision to kill. With the serial killer, the motivation typically arises within the psyche of the sequential murderer. The motivation often centers around a sexual motivation and the sexual gratification that will be realized when the murder occurs. In *Serial Murder* (Holmes and Holmes, 1998a), the authors stated that the serial killer who is of the lust, thrill, or power/control type will murder in an elongated fashion, a *process-focused* murder. By drawing out the torture, humiliation, and so on, of the helpless victim, the killer receives some form of perverse gratification from the murder or from acting out the fantasy. The fantasy may precede, accompany, or follow the murder. It is not a blitz attack, an *act-focused* murder. By the *process of the murder* the killer is able to achieve immense pleasure and gratification, usually of a sexual nature.

However, with a mass killer of the family annihilator type, this person murders family members for reasons that are part of his own psyche. The motivation(s) lies within his own psychological makeup, not with the commandments of others as with the disciple mass murderer. There is nothing outside his psyche that commands his decision to kill.

Anticipated Gain: ***The anticipated gain is expressive or psychological.*** What does the family annihilator wish to gain from the murder of those within his family? The overwhelming number of cases in which this type of mass killer is involved appears to be an expressive or psychological gain. Of course, there are obvious exceptions. In a few cases, for example, a family member may kill other members for material gain. There are monies to be realized, for example, in the form of insurance, business interests, and so on, if certain family members are dead. But this appears to be the exception rather than the rule. This type of murder usually involves only one member of the family, usually the spouse of the killer. The family annihilator kills family members for various reasons, intrinsic in nature, and the gain is psychological. This certainly was the case in the List and Simmons murder cases. List is discussed in more detail in a subsequent case study.

In the MacDonald case, it is difficult to ascertain exactly the anticipated gain, since MacDonald has consistently maintained his innocence. There are some who believe that he wanted to live a different lifestyle than that of being "burdened" by a wife and children. Or he may have been in love with another woman, the murder being the only way he could be free of his wife and marry again (McGinnis, 1985). In other cases, it may be easier to develop a reason for the fatal actions. With John List, as we shall see later, the anticipated gain was easier to determine.

Victim Selectivity: ***The victims are selected on a nonrandom basis.*** The victims of the family annihilator are not random; there is a relationship between the killer and his victims. In this case, the killer knows the victims: wives, children, parents, and other close relations. We witnessed this in the Jeffrey MacDonald case. The wife and the two daughters were the intended victims. The killer and his victims were obviously in close proximity. They all lived in the same home and interacted daily. This is not true for other types of mass killers and their victims. The victims of the Manson family were unknown to the killers.

Case Study

Jeffrey MacDonald

On February 17, 1970, the military police at Fort Bragg, North Carolina, were called to the home of Green Beret Army Captain Jeffrey MacDonald. MacDonald phoned the police to inform them that his family had been killed. When the police arrived, the apartment was a scene of carnage. In three separate bedrooms, the bodies of his wife, Collete, age 26, Kimberly, age 5, and Kristen, age 2, were found brutally and savagely murdered. MacDonald, alive but wounded, was found lying beside the body of his wife. His wounds were relatively minor, and he quickly recovered from his injuries (Potter and Bost, 1997).

The rooms inside the MacDonald apartment were devoid of signs of a struggle. On one headboard in the girl's bedroom, "pig" was written in blood. Captain MacDonald stated that a group of young hippies, three men and one woman, came into his home while he was sleeping on the couch. They were chanting "acid is groovy" and "kill the pigs." He emphasized that the woman was wearing a huge, floppy hat and was carrying a candle. He said he fought with the intruders but was overcome. He was then stabbed. After this initial attack upon him, the intruders went into the other rooms, where they killed his daughters and wife.

Initially, the community at the Army post was sympathetic with MacDonald. Upon further investigation, MacDonald quickly became the prime suspect. The physical evidence, the clothing worn by the victims and the bloodstains, was submitted to the Federal Bureau of Investigation for examination. The experts testified in court that the pattern of knife entry in the wife's gown could not have come from her in the manner MacDonald explained. The pattern of knife wounds could only have come if the clothing were folded, unlike the normal pattern of someone wearing a robe. The robe would have had to lain on a flat surface, not have been worn.

A year passed. The Army Criminal Investigation Unit informed the federal prosecutors that the evidence still pointed toward MacDonald as the prime suspect. (This was a federal crime since the murder occurred on a federal military base.) Finally, in 1975, MacDonald was brought to trial, based primarily on circumstantial evidence. The jury found him guilty of murder in the first degree of his wife and of murder in the second degree of his two daughters. He received three consecutive life sentences.

In 1980, an appeal was heard by the U. S. Fourth Circuit Court of Appeals. The court set aside the verdict of five years earlier on the basis that MacDonald's rights were violated on the grounds that he was not granted a speedy trial. In 1983, the U. S. Supreme Court set aside the ruling of the Circuit Court of Appeals and MacDonald was returned to prison to serve his sentence. MacDonald's case is still under appeal.

Source: The material in this case study was obtained from Cox et al. (1991, pp. 238–239), McGinnis (1985), and Potter and Bost (1992).

This victim selectivity process is not a big surprise. The victims are carefully selected from all other victims. They are chosen because of who they are, family members. They are not innocent lunch customers at a fast-food restaurant. They are chosen simply because of the relationship with the victim. In Ankeny, Iowa,

Larry Buttz, who had been only recently charged with domestic violence, went in his home and killed his wife, Delane, age 38, and their children, Ryan, 15, and Lindsey, 12 (*Courier-Journal*, Louisville, KY, November 6, 1996, p. A2). The victims were not selected randomly. They were chosen because of their status as the wife and the children of the killer. In another case, Lawrence DeLisle, age 28, intentionally drove his car into the Detroit River with the manifest purpose of drowning his wife and four children. The children, Brian, 8, Melissa, 4, Kasdie, 2, and Emily, 8 months, all died; the wife survived. DeLisle stated that he wanted to kill his family so that he would be free of them (*Courier-Journal*, Louisville, KY, November 6, 1996, p. A2). Again, what are the characteristics of the victims other than being members of his family? The answer is simple: none.

Victim Relationship: ***The victims are related, usually family members.*** From the discussion above, it is apparent that there is a close personal and spatial relationship between the family annihilator and the victims. This is apparent in the cases that have already been discussed. DeLisle wanted to kill his wife and children so that he would be free of their demands. James Colbert, age 39, was dissuaded by police from jumping off a bridge in Concord, New Hampshire. He allegedly strangled his wife and smothered his three children. He called the police and said that he had just killed his wife and children (*Courier-Journal*, Louisville, KY, October 28, 1996, p. A2).

On October 2, 1997, 20-year-old Timothy Prink was charged with the shotgun slaying of four members of his adoptive family. The reason? He said the family members were calling him names and treating him with no respect (*Courier-Journal*, Louisville, KY, October 3, 1997, p. A2). He has not been tried as the time of this writing. In Lowell, Massachusetts, a married U. S. National Guard technical sergeant killed his girlfriend and their two children. Peter Contos, 31, was arrested for their murder after the body of his girlfriend was found by a neighbor. He had driven back to the military base with the bodies of the two boys, 4 years and 2 months, in his car. He then placed them into his locker. He had a wife, but the wife and the girlfriend were not aware of the other's existence. What did the victims have in common? They were acquainted with the killer.

Spatial Mobility: ***The killer is usually a long-time resident of the community.*** The family annihilator is usually a person who has been a lifelong resident of a community. The killer has been educated in this hometown, often employed there, and is often known widely by those in the community and neighborhood. There is no need for the family annihilator to go from one location to another in a search for potential and vulnerable victims. The victims live in his own household; they are members of his own family. Sometimes, the victims are relatives who live outside his home (e.g., his parents, grandparents, and other relatives) but reside closeby, in the same neighborhood or at least in the same community. Unlike the disciple killer and the set-and-run killer, the family annihilator has no need to travel to select and kill victims.

Case Study

John List

In the late evening—early morning hours of December 7, 1972, the police were alerted that there had been a multiple murder in the home of John List. Four bodies were found in the ballroom of the List household: Helen, the wife, and the three children, Patty, John, Jr., and Frederick. List's mother, Alma, was found in a closet on the third floor, where she had her own apartment. The police searched the house cautiously. They were not certain if the killer was still in the house and if they still had to find a sixth victim, John List. In the basement, they found the family dog, Tinkerbelle. It had also been killed.

Who could have done such a tragic thing? What kind of human monster could have taken the life of five members of a family and then simply vanish? These questions would not be answered for 17 years.

John was the only child of his parents, J. F. and Alma List. He was a loner. Born in 1925, his dictatorial upbringing by his mother, and the family's strict and fanatical adherence to the Lutheran religion, produced a child who was not only lonely but dedicated to family values, a belief that God will provide, and a belief that if one works hard enough, there are tangible rewards in this life. He had few friends in his Lutheran elementary school, and his mother would not permit him any friends of whom she did not approve. Childhood playmates would have to come to the List home; John was not allowed to stray where the mother would not be there to supervise and check on him. Friends would later say that Mrs. List would check on her son at least once every 15 fifteen minutes to make certain that everything was well.

As John grew, he was considered a loner in his secular high school. He was not involved in extracurricular activities. He was studious and was an honor student. After high school, he enlisted in the army and rose to the rank of sergeant. After World War II, he enrolled at the University of Michigan and earned a degree in business, and only three months later was granted an M.B.A.

After graduation, he developed a few friendships with other men. One night at a bowling alley, he noticed a beautiful young woman. After a short dating period, they became engaged. Helen was a widow and mother to an 8-year-old daughter, Brenda. Her first husband died in the Korean War. He led a group of soldiers into battle and was awarded the Silver Cross. In the times that he spent apart from Helen during their marriage, he contracted a sexually transmitted disease and passed it on to Helen. The venereal disease became so debilitating to her that it prevented her from fulfilling her responsibilities as wife and mother.

As the time for their marriage approached, Helen announced to John that she was pregnant. He consented to marry her despite some ambivalent feelings about whether he truly loved her. Despite these feelings, John decided to go on with the wedding. The night before they were to be married, she confessed to John that she was not pregnant. Nevertheless, he decided to go ahead with the wedding. Later, he would say many times that he regretted this decision.

During their early married years, John and Helen encountered numerous financial setbacks. Finally, after having three children, a girl and two boys, the family decided that they needed to make a move to New Jersey, where John was hired as vice president at a local bank. The top priority for List at the bank was to design a computer data set to identify customers and financial problems. In the time that he was there, barely more than a year, he was unable to accomplish this task but had gotten the family heavily in debt. His mortgage on a dilapidated mansion, the food bill, clothing, utilities, and even the milk bill became monthly costs that he could no longer meet. To make matters worse, List was then fired from his job.

Neighbors believed John to be a odd person. For example, he cut his grass in a shirt and tie, often even in a business suit. He had few social outlets. His activities at home consisted of chores around the house, reading the Bible, and playing board games with a military theme. Helen became more ill, and hospitalization was recommended for an illness that had been exacerbated by the venereal disease and her progressive alcoholism. She spent more time confined to bed. The household was maintained by John and the children, especially their daughter, Patty.

Patty was now a teenager. She became involved in the drama club, but soon her grades dropped, perhaps because of her alleged involvement in the occult, satanism, and recreational drugs. List chaffed at his daughter's rejection of the religious tenets of Lutheranism. He wanted her to return to his very restricted way of living. Helen was of no help in the family's life. The two sons were only minor problems. John's time at home centered around Helen, Patty, and financial survival. All the while, employment and financial problems were enveloping John. After being fired from his job at the bank, he secured employment as an insurance salesman, but this too resulted in a loss of income and further financial distress.

List must have debated the best way to rid himself of the impending doom of financial ruin. His religion taught him that God would not let him fail. His religion also demanded that he follow certain rules in order to be saved. To resolve his problems in the days before he killed his family, John List examined his options. He could kill himself, but this was not a feasible option since his belief was that he could not go to heaven if he committed suicide. He could divorce his wife, but the Bible and his Lutheran faith had precepts against this practice: "What God has joined together, let no man put asunder." His third option, killing his family, finally emerged as the favored option. If he were to kill his family, his wife and children would go to heaven and he could be forgiven by God since he believed that there is no sin that God will not forgive. After all, John had done all he could to provide for his family, but that was not apparently in God's plan. So the best plan was for John to murder his family.

On the morning of November 7, 1971, John sent the children off to school. After they had left, John killed his wife, then leisurely moved her body to the ballroom at the rear of the house. He placed her on a sleeping bag with a cover partially hiding part of her body but exposing her hips and genital area. A cloth was placed over her face. He then went upstairs to the third floor, where he killed his mother. He left her on the third floor hallway because, as he would later admit, she was too heavy to move to the first floor. He then called his daughter home from school under the pretext that the family was going out of town to visit Helen's mother, who was very ill. This ruse worked to get both Patricia and his two sons out of school. Patricia was the first child killed. As she entered the house her father killed her with one shot to her head. Then the two sons came home, one at a time, and they were also murdered. The three children were then all moved into the ballroom, where they were placed in a position of repose perpendicular to their mother. The children were wearing heavy winter coats and gloves. John, the older son, was lying on his back. Frederick, the youngest, was in the middle, face down. Patricia was on the end, almost in a fetal position, facing her brothers.

John had already eaten breakfast and lunch, and he would leave the house and disappear later that evening. According to his methodological mind, he had stopped the newspaper and the mail, and had informed neighbors that he was leaving town with his family for a visit to Helen's sick mother. The only item that was not stopped temporarily was a monthly newsletter that served this small community. List also left the lights on in the house, something he had not done before because of the cost. He also turned down the furnace, and the cold temperature delayed decomposition of the bodies inside the house. When the bodies were found a month later, they were remarkably well preserved.

John List then effectively disappeared for the next 17 years. In effect, List simply moved to Denver, where he changed his name to Robert Clark. For the next 17 years, he would live a secret life. He worked in the same field, accounting, and was successful in finding jobs with various employers in the Denver area. He became active in several Lutheran churches in the Denver area. Church members remembered that List could be counted on to lend his expertise to financial matters. He also volunteered for other committees and was considered a valued member of the church community. He met a woman, Delores, and after courting for almost six years, they married in 1985 in Maryland, the same state in which he and Helen had married years earlier. They were married in the local Lutheran church.

As happened so often, List lost his jobs with several employers. He and his new wife decided to relocate to Virginia. There he secured new employment and developed several friends, especially a neighbor and his wife. It seemed that the years were treating List better. He appeared to relax his guard. His announcement that his first wife died of cancer and that he had no children were readily accepted. There were no other meaningful inquiries into his background. He had been able successfully to hide his past. He had secured a new Social Security card and other important governmental documents. But the end was drawing near for John List. A neighbor and a friend of Delores's brought over to the Clark household an article with a picture of what John List would look like after almost 20 years. The neighbor showed the article and picture to Mrs. Clark, who quickly dismissed the notion that it was her husband and threw the tabloid away. The same neighbor called the *America's Most Wanted* TV program to report the whereabouts of John List, whom she knew as Joseph Clark. On May 1, 1989, *America's Most Wanted* presented a short segment on the List case. Millions of people witnessed the broadcast and there were more than 300 telephone calls as a result of the presentation.

A month later, two FBI agents went to the Clark home. Mrs. Clark was home but her husband was at work. The agents questioned Mrs. Clark and became convinced that she did not know the true identity of her husband. She informed them of Clark's employer's name, and the agents arrested List at work. He offered no resistance.

John List went to trial for the murder of his wife, mother, and three children. He was found guilty on all accounts and was given five consecutive life sentences that all but guaranteed that he will be in prison for the rest of his life.

Source: Information on the John List murder case was obtained from Benford and Johnson (1991), Ryzuk (1990), and Sharkey (1990).

Some family annihilators do leave the scene of the crime and move to a new location where they are not known. In this respect, the killer is attempting to escape detection and apprehension. This is the scenario followed by John List.

At the time of sentencing List stated that he was sorry for the trouble and suffering that he had caused but did not appear to have any sorrow for the murder of his family. Perhaps in his convoluted sense of values, he believes that his family is in a better place, a place where Helen is free of her disease and addiction, a place where his mother suffers no longer from the illnesses that old age invariably brings, a place where Patricia will not be exposed to the temptations of drugs, satanism, and sex, and where the two sons, John, Jr. and Frederick, will not be placed in situations where failure is a possibility regardless of how hard one works. Nevertheless, there are five dead family members, innocent victims of a man who could not live up to the expectations of his mother, his religion, and probably most important his own measure of his successes (few in number) and his failures (insurmountable in his own evaluation).

Victim Traits: ***The traits of the victims are unimportant to the killer.*** Physical traits are unimportant to the mass killer. The victims are all acquaintances of the killer, but no particular physical traits are necessary for a decision to kill. This is true for all family annihilators since they kill those who are members of their direct family, close family members, and in some cases, distant relatives who may not even live with the killer prior to the mass murder.

CONCLUSION

The family annihilator is the most common type of mass killer, one that appears most often in newscasts and radio broadcasts. Perhaps it is the one most difficult to understand. What would impel Ronald Gene Simmons to kill two strangers and 14 family members? Are they the same influences that commanded John List to kill his family? We think not. However, until we can determine exactly the psychological causes for mass murder in general and family annihilation in particular, there can be no clear statement of causation.

What can be done, however, is to make society aware that certain behavioral cues might alert us to a person who may develop into a mass killer. With Simmons, the isolation that he placed around himself and his family, the sexual pathology that manifested itself as incest, and his hostility and unwanted sexual advances may have been behavioral cues. With List, the inability to keep jobs, the strict adherence to dogmatic rules of organized religion, the inability or unwillingness to become a social being, and again the social isolation of the family as dictated by the killer may be indicators of future problems that may include family annihilation. With this awareness may come identification of potential at-risk families. Interdiction may be indicated, resulting in the prevention of needless deaths.

Nevertheless, there will continue to be cases like Simmons and List. There are still social and individual causes that will compel people with pathological personalities to commit the most atrocious of all acts, the killing of one's own family.

Discussion Questions

1. How is the family annihilator different from other types of mass murderers? How does he or she select victims?

2. What are the apparent motivations of the family annihilator? What is the anticipated gain from the kill? Does the killer remain geographically stable? What do victims of this type of murderer have in common?

3. What role does sexual gratification or humiliation of the victim play in the murderous acts of family annihilators? How is this different in serial killers?

4. List three specific examples of mass murderers that could be labeled family annihilators.

5. Why do you believe that the family annihilator is thought to be the most common type of mass killer?

CHAPTER 6

The Disgruntled Employee Mass Killer

In March 1995, Christopher Green, a former postal worker, killed two former co-workers and two customers. Green said that he was trying to hold up the post office because he was deeply in debt.

In April 1995, James Simpson started the day by killing his wife. Simpson, a refinery worker, then walked into his company's plant, where he killed his former boss and three fellow workers. Simpson, from Corpus Christi, Texas, then walked out of the plant and shot himself. He died later that day.

A former San Diego State University graduate student, Frederick Martin Davidson, killed three engineering university faculty members who were also members of his thesis committee. Davidson stated that he believed that all three members of his committee were conspiring to keep him from securing a good job. He received three life sentences.

INTRODUCTION

What went through the mind of David Burke will never be known. Fired as an employee from Pacific Southwest Airlines, he boarded a plane following his ex-boss. As the plane was on its way to its destination, Burke shot and killed his boss, caused the airplane to crash, and killed 43 people on board, including himself. In Mississippi, Kenneth Tornes, a firefighter, returned to his firehouse one evening. He killed four supervisors before he was wounded in a gunfight with police. In California, Willie Woods, a Los Angeles electrician, went to his workplace and shot and killed two supervisors and two fellow employees. He was arrested at the crime scene by two police officers who happened to be in the area. On April 3, 1995, James Simpson walked into the oil refinery where he once worked and killed his wife, former boss, and three other employees. He then walked out the back door and killed himself.

Another disgruntled employee who killed is Joseph Harris, 35. A former postal worker, Harris had a reputation of simply disliking people. His co-workers stated that it did not make any difference if you were male or female, black or white—Harris disliked everyone. Originally hired in 1981, Harris worked for the

U.S. Postal Service in 1990, when he was fired for refusing to cooperate in an investigation of charges brought against him by a former supervisor, Carol Ott.

In the early morning hours of October 9, 1991, Harris walked into the back door of the post office in Ridgewood, New Jersey. He apparently had a key that was given to mail sorters, his former job. He killed two employees of the post office. Several hours before, he had gone to Ott's home dressed in a bulletproof vest and armed with two submachine guns, grenades, and a sword. He slashed her to death and shot and killed her fiancé, Cornelius Kasten, Jr. Ott was partly disrobed, and Kasten was found in a chair in front of the TV set, shot once in the head.

Harris was apprehended in the post office after hiding for almost five hours. He had left a note at his home that he shared with his mother. The note contained information illustrating his dissatisfaction with the post office. He believed that he was not treated fairly and used his act of mass murder to express his anger and exert revenge on innocent people.

More than 30 years ago, Robert Earl Mack was fired from his job at General Dynamics, a defense contractor. Mack was 42 years old and had worked for the company for 25 years. In his last year there, fellow employees noted a change in Mack's work habits and personality. He began to show up late and then, to miss days of work. He was fired. Nine days after he was fired, Mack was scheduled to appear before an appeals board. During a break in the meeting, Mack opened fire on his former co-workers. He then surrendered to local authorities.

See Table 6.1 for other disgruntled employee mass killers.

TRAITS OF THE DISGRUNTLED EMPLOYEE MASS KILLER

Violence committed in the workplace usually takes one of three forms:

1. Those committed by people who work at the place where the crime took place
2. Those committed by people who are or were customers of the business at which the violence took place
3. Those committed by people who have no relationship with the business or company involved

In examining these three forms of mass murder in the workplace committed by disgruntled employees, it is apparent that many of these crimes are committed by those who have some type of relationship with the company (Seger, 1993). One, Frederick Davidson, killed three members of his thesis committee. On first glance, this may not appear to fit the traits or characteristics of a disgruntled employee mass killer. However, upon closer examination, a case can be made that this killer was a "customer" of the university, and that Davidson was to receive a product, a degree. He believed that the university was negligent in not assisting him in his employment endeavors as well as in delaying in granting him a degree.

TABLE 6.1   Selected Alleged and Suspected Disgruntled Employee Mass Killers

Name	State	Victims
Matthew Beck	Connecticut	Killed 4 co-workers
David Burk	California	Killed 43 people in an airplane
Gerald Clemons	Ohio	Killed 3 people at his former workplace
Frederick Davidson	California	Killed 3 members of his thesis committee
James Davis	North Carolina	Killed 3 co-workers
Gian Ferri	California	Killed 6 people in his attorney's office
Christopher Green	California	Killed 4 people at a post office
Joseph Harris	New Jersey	Killed 4 people at a post office
Richard Herr	Delaware	Killed 3 co-workers
Eric Houston	California	Killed 4 people at his former high school
Kenneth Jones	Mississippi	Killed his wife and four co-workers
Clifton McCree	Florida	Killed 5 fellow workers
James Simpson	Texas	Killed his wife, boss, and three co-workers
Kenneth Tornes	Mississippi	Killed his wife and 4 co-workers
Joseph Wesbecker	Kentucky	Shot 7 people at his workplace
Willie Woods	California	Killed 4 co-workers

Other cases are clearer. Joseph Harris, for example, went into his place of former employment, a post office, and killed four co-workers. Joseph Wesbecker did the same when he returned to the Standard Gravure Printing Co. looking for supervisors who were, in Wesbecker's mind, responsible for his disability leave.

The disgruntled employee mass killer has certain traits that are fundamentally different from those of other types of mass killers (See Table 6.2).

Motivation: ***The motivation is intrinsic to the personality of the disgruntled mass killer.*** The motivation to kill innocent persons who fall prey to a disgruntled mass killer lies within the psyche of the killer (O'Boyle, 1992; Roth, 1994). There are no motivations that arise from outside the personality of the offender. Witness again the case of Harris. He was often belittled by his co-workers (Losey, 1994). He ascribed the blame for all of his problems outside his own arena of responsibility. The motivation to kill, however, rested within his personality.

Anticipated Gain: ***The anticipated gain is expressive.*** The disgruntled employee expects some reward for his act of mass murder. This anticipated gain is expressive or psychological. The gain is somewhat difficult for most people to understand. How could the killing of innocent persons, many of whom were workplace associates, be psychologically pleasurable? For the disgruntled employee, this question is easy to address. From the actions of one episodic act of homicide, the

TABLE 6.2 Traits of the Disgruntled Employee Mass Killer

Motivation
  Intrinsic
  Extrinsic
	The motivation is intrinsic to the personality of the killer.

Anticipated gain
  Expressive
  Instrumental
	An expressive or psychological gain is anticipated by the killer.

Victim selectivity
  Random
  Nonrandom
	The victims are former or current fellow employees; usually selected at random.

Victim relationship
  Affiliative
  Strangers
	The victims are typically not related to the killer; they are strangers, although many were known as fellow workers.

Spatial mobility
  Stable
  Transient
	The disgruntled employee is typically a geographically stable person.

Victim traits
  Specific
  Nonspecific
	Physical traits are not important to this type of mass killer. Victims are simply in the wrong place at the wrong time.

attention is called not only to the person committing the act but also to the occurrences that brought about the killings. Of course, these occurrences are primarily in the mind of the killer (intrinsic motivation), but they add substance to the motivation as well as drawing attention to injustices that brought about the killing. Maybe this is a rationalization for the killings: a denial of injury, a denial of victims, and a denial of responsibility (Sykes and Matza, 1957).

Victim Selectivity: ***The victims are randomly selected.*** In the case of disgruntled employees, the victims are often former co-workers of the killer. In the case of Joseph Harris, the two employees and the former supervisor came into contact with the man almost daily. As a mail sorter for the post office, he would be there interacting daily with other workers despite his abrasive attitude and personality. When he selected his victims at the workplace, the two just happened to be at the wrong place at the wrong time. Thus victims are selected at random.

We need to clarify the randomness of victim selection. True, the victims are often co-workers or former co-workers. But when this mass killer enters the place of employment, victims are usually selected simply because they are in the view of the killer. The disgruntled employee killer may enter the facility seeking a specific target (e.g., a former supervisor), but kill others with no predetermined selection

Case Study

Joseph Wesbecker

On Thursday, September 14, 1989, at approximately 8:30 A.M., a disturbed and angry man went to his former place of employment. He had been placed on disability leave seven months previously for severe psychiatric problems. He was armed with an AK-47, clips of ammunition, a SIG-Sauer 9mm semiautomatic assault pistol, a MAC-11 semiautomatic pistol, a bayonet, a .38-caliber Smith & Wesson revolver, a second MAC-11, and several hundred rounds of ammunition. The MAC-11s had been purchased only four days before. Joseph Wesbecker stepped onto the elevator of the Standard Gravure Printing Co. in Louisville, his former employer of over 20 years. When he walked from the elevator onto the third floor, Sharon Needy, age 49, a receptionist, was standing talking with another employee. She had gotten to work a little early that day to attend to some business that needed extra attention and planned to compensate by taking an extended lunch hour. She was the first one shot as Wesbecker opened fire. Her husband, George, said that he was told by the police that Wesbecker started shooting as soon as he stepped out of the elevator. Sharon happened to be at another workstation, not her own (personal interview, May 10, 1998).

Weapons that Joseph Wesbecker took inside the printing company. (Courtesy of the Louisville Police Department)

Receptionist desk across from the elevator where Joseph Wesbecker exited and started his act of mass murder. (Courtesy of the Louisville Police Department)

Lt. Jeff Moody, with the homicide unit of the Louisville Police Department, was one of the first police officers to respond to the scene. He reported that when the police entered the plant, they found blood and bodies scattered around the building. Moreover, they were not uncertain where Wesbecker was. After Wesbecker shot Needy, he shot another receptionist, Angela Bowman, who survived. Walking through the hallways, Wesbecker fired randomly at anyone he saw. A few workers gathered together in one office and escaped his detection. One worker, lying on the floor, heard some shots and then there was silence. She dialed 911. The call went through the telephone system at 8:38 A.M. Within the next minute, more than a dozen more calls went through the 911 system, calls asking for aid and protection from a crazed killer who was stalking the premises of the plant.

Wesbecker continued his killings. He encountered one fellow worker, a casual acquaintance, and told him to get away from him. Why Wesbecker did not shoot this man was unclear. By this time, word had circulated throughout the plant that Crazy Joe Wesbecker (Holmes and Holmes, 1998a) was shooting people. Many ran and escaped his uncontrolled rage.

Walking down the hallway into the bindery division, he shot and killed James Husband, 47. He walked through a tunnel and down to the ground floor where he shot and killed William Gannet, 46, James Wile, 56, and Lloyd White, 42. In the basement, Wesbecker killed Richard Bragger, 54, and Paul Sale, 60. Wesbecker shot 13 other workers, but fortunately they survived. The last shot was fired when Wesbecker took his own life in the pressroom on the ground floor only a short distance from Wile, one of the victims. He shot himself in the face with one of his pistols.

What kind of man would go into his place of employment of two decades and kill people who bore no culpability for his medical disability termination? There is no clear answer. But we do know that this was a carefully planned case of mass murder. Wesbecker started collecting his weapons about a year earlier. Did he start planning his rampage a year before?

"Has this been a plotted, methodically planned situation that he finally brought to culmination, or did something happen to him to set him off? We haven't been able to find that," said Louisville homicide detective Sgt. Gene Waldridge, who has been interviewing Wesbecker's relatives and looking into his background.

Police, who said Wesbecker suffered from manic depression, still plan to interview a psychiatrist he had been seeing, as well as at least 40 Standard Gravure workers, including Wesbecker's former bosses.

But Waldridge said: "The big question—Why?—more than likely will never, ever be answered. You can't talk to that person. You don't know what motivates them..." (*Courier-Journal*, Louisville, KY, September 16, 1989, p. A1)

There were special stressors that compelled Wesbecker to shoot 20 people and then end his own life. Wesbecker had been seeking psychiatric help for the past year. He was a patient in psychotherapy as well as drug therapy. Years later, relatives of the victims would sue the makers of Prozac, Wesbecker's drug, and claim that it caused him to become a mass killer. The suit was judged in favor of the drug company.

Wesbecker, age 47, was apparently tormented by his dismissal from work. He thought that the company failed to compensate him for the time and the stress that he had undergone on their behalf. He was angry at supervisors, and he told one fellow employee that he would "blow out the brains" of any supervisor who came up to him (*Courier-Journal*, Louisville, KY, October 1, 1989, p. A1). Wesbecker told other employees that he had thought about hiring someone to kill some of the people at the plant. He also

The docking area and elevator inside the Standard Grauvre Printing Co. Joseph Wesbecker killed another victim at this site. (Courtesy of the Louisville Police Department)

related that he had plans to operate a remote control model airplane with plastic explosives that he would guide through the plant to a determined destination. He also told a fellow worker, "Me and old ack-ack will do a job that's been long overdue" (ibid., p. A16). Some workers acknowledged later that they should have taken his threats more seriously. He had a list of people who he wanted dead. That list included the executive vice-president of the company as well as the owner of the company. As one employee said: "You just figure he was mad at management. You figure it's just a way to get your frustration and your stress out....You don't take it seriously" (ibid.). Another worker said that another employee told him about Wesbecker's explosive plan. He quickly dismissed the idea that Wesbecker was a real and present danger. He added, "I really didn't think he'd ever do anything....I'm sure you've had people you work with talk about meeting a guy outside, punching him out or whatever. Well, maybe one out of every two or three hundred it might happen. But most of the time a guy thinks about it five or 10 minutes and wonders why he ever made such a dumb remark" (ibid.).

The threats made by Wesbecker to his fellow workers were never made known to the supervisors at the plant. Although his remarks were common knowledge to the people in the factory, the general manager, plant manager, vice-president of operations, and other managerial personnel were unaware of the extent of the problem. This made Wesbecker's eventual action more than a real possibility. There could have been legal proscriptions barring Wesbecker from the premises or other legal orders that could possibly have circumvented an action that resulted in 20 innocent people

The receptionist area where Joseph Wesbecker killed his first two victims. (Courtesy of the Louisville Police Department)

shot and seven killed. Additionally, an argument can be made against the fellow workers, who should have taken his comments more seriously and made them available to those who could have taken legal action.

Wesbecker is buried with his parents in a small Catholic cemetery in southern Indiana. His gravestone overlooks a peaceful valley among those of many early settlers in Elizabeth, Indiana: the Browns, Finks, Johns, and others. St. Peter's Catholic Church held the mass of burial for this mass killer. The priest asked for forgiveness of the act of this "troubled" man and a belief in the divine plan of God. But perhaps society needs more of its own plan, so that other innocent victims do not meet the same end. Early identification of troubled employees, psychological services given to needful employees, and other human services could provide important human contacts that might prevent the murder of innocent victims.

process. Fatal violence is directed toward people in the workplace who are working that day (Bensimon, 1994). The killer may be looking for a supervisor, but that does not preclude the murderer from killing others at the scene.

Victim Relationship: ***The victims are not related to the killer.*** The victims of a disgruntled employee are typically not related to the killer by blood or by marriage. They are strangers to the killer's family; the only ties are those they all share by working in the same facility. For example, in March 1995, Christopher Green, another former postal worker, went back to his former place of employment and killed two fellow employees and two customers. His reason was that he was in debt and the post office owed him some past wages.

In the case used as a case study later in the chapter, Joseph Wesbecker had been employed with the same company for over 20 years. Certainly, he knew somewhat well some of the people he worked with during those years. However, all admitted that they had never been to Wesbecker's home, and none knew the killer on a personal level; he was simply a fellow employee. They all felt Wesbecker was strange and that his behavior bordered on the weird. None admitted to having personal ties with him. Wesbecker fits the profile of the disgruntled employee. A loner on medication for his mental illness, with an inordinate interest in weapons and a grudge against the administrators at his former place of employment because of his involuntary separation, Wesbecker ended his own life and thus prevented further investigation into his psyche seeking answers to important questions.

Spatial Mobility: ***The killer tends to be geographically stable. He or she lives and works in a community for long periods of time.*** The disgruntled employee is typically a geographically stable mass killer. He or she has roots in the community, family, worship center, recreational interests, and employment. This was the case both for Joseph Harris, who killed in the post office, and for Joseph Wesbecker.

This killer usually has community ties and has worked a long period of time in his or her place of employment. Over time, the killer has built up a sense of anomie, hate, and revenge. He or she acts out of this sense of rage. Table 6.3 covers various levels of violence in the workplace which may be shown by a disgruntled employee. As can be seen from the progression of personal violence in the table, it is apparent that such a person is usually a long-term employee. It takes some time for the employee to build up to the point where violent fatal behavior is manifested.

Victim Traits: **Physical traits are unimportant to the killer.** The disgruntled employee does not kill for sexual reasons. He or she kills because the anticipated gain is psychological and the reason or motivation is intrinsic to the personality of the killer. He or she does not, as does the lust serial killer, seek out an ideal victim type who embodies certain physical traits, such as hair style or color, body build, or other physical attributes. The lust killer murders for

---

TABLE 6.3   Levels of Personal Violence in the Workplace

Level 1

- Refuses to cooperate with immediate supervisor
- Spreads rumors and gossip to harm others
- Consistently argues with co-workers
- Belligerent toward customers or clients
- Consistently swears at others
- Makes unwelcome sexual comments

Level 2

- Argues increasingly with customers, vendors, co-workers, and management
- Refuses to obey company policies and procedures
- Sabotages equipment and steals property for revenge
- Verbalizes wishes to hurt co-workers and/or management
- Sends sexual or violent notes to co-workers and/or management
- Sees self as victimized by management (a "me against them" mentality)

Level 3
Frequent displays of intense anger, resulting in:
- Recurrent suicidal threats
- Recurrent physical fights
- Destruction of property
- Utilization of weapons to harm others
- Commission of murder, rape, and/or arson

Source: Adapted from Baron (1993).

completely different reasons. The disgruntled employee killer murders because of perceived injustice.

The physical characteristics of the victims are inconsequential. They are simply in a place where a mass killing occurs. A victim is killed because he or she shares the physical space of the killer. There is no personal relationship. There is only a sense of happenstance. In the case of the disgruntled employee, the victim happens to be a fellow employee. In the case of the disgruntled citizen (Chapter 9), the victim happens to be a customer or shares the space with the killer. Attractiveness, body build, and so on, play no role in the victimization in either case.

CONCLUSION

There is no completely effective plan that will protect us from the acts of a disgruntled employee. Such a mass killer will randomly select victims from those who shared his or her own space in the workplace, although there is no affinity between the killer and the victim. The victims are either complete strangers or know the killer only as a fellow worker. If the killer knows a potential victim in this scenario, as was the case with Wesbecker, the killer will sometimes spare that person's life.

Among all cases of mass killers, the disgruntled employee is perhaps the most visible. Such cases generally capture the headlines. Our research for this book shows that family annihilators murder more victims but that most of the time, these murders are not reported on the front pages of newspapers. Nevertheless, both types of mass killers will continue to commit their acts of senseless killing.

A possible proactive strategy is to develop a policy within a company or agency that a troubled employee would be encouraged to follow if the company suspects that there is a person who presents a danger. Employee education is an important part of any company's plan to prevent the mass murder of its most important asset, its employees.

Discussion Questions

1. Why do you believe that the prevalence of disgruntled employees who later become mass murderers goes in cycles? What is it about large agencies or governmental bureaucracies that makes them more frequent victims of disgruntled employee mass murderers?

2. What type of gain does a disgruntled employee expect to receive after having committed his or her murderous deed?

3. Why do you believe that during commission of the act, the disgruntled employee often is not as concerned with murdering specific persons who may have ridiculed him or her in the past, but is most concerned with taking the lives of persons within a branch or department of the agency?

4. List and describe the three levels of personal violence in the workplace. How may a typology like this be useful for management and both governmental and nongovernmental policymakers?

5. What role do the physical traits of the victim play in killings by disgruntled employee mass murderers?

CHAPTER 7

The Ideological Mass Killer

On March 11, 1997, a lone gunman, reciting the Lord's Prayer and holding everyone in a bank hostage, killed two bank employees, and then walking outside, shot an elderly man in the back of the head, killing him. The name of the killer was Allen Griffin, Jr., age 21. Although we will never know the exact motivation for this mass killing, there was a religious overtone to his killings.

In a small town in Ohio, Susan Luff was sentenced to prison for a charge of conspiracy to commit aggravated murder. Another cult member, Richard Brand, was sent to prison for five counts of aggravated murder. The two young followers of cult leader Jeffrey Lundgren were sentenced in connection with the deaths of a husband, wife, and three children who were also members of the Lundgren cult.

INTRODUCTION

When there is an act of mass murder, there is an immediate but often short-lived community outcry. When the victims are children, such as in the Oklahoma City bombing case, the outcry is heard across the nation. Children are often the victims of mass murder when the act occurs in a public place such as a restaurant, public building, or similar locations, as in the case of Timothy McVeigh. The youth of the victims in the day care center of the Murrah Federal Building in Oklahoma City made this crime all the more heinous.

With the ideological mass killer, there are no innocents. The victims are considered to be "collateral damage." They are victims of war. Many Americans recall the horror of the Olympic athletes killed by a explosion during the games in Germany. Certainly, those victims, the athletes, were not warriors in battle other than in the games themselves. But the ideology of this type of killer demands the lives of those who fall within a targeted area. What is the philosophy of the ideological mass killer? If the act is one of mass murder and the motivation may be political, Netter (1982, pp. 228–237) offers the following:

1. *No rules*. Terrorists differ from soldiers in war and police action in that terrorists consciously violate all conventions.

2. *No innocents.* The "unjust system" includes a fight against all people within that system who do not side with them.

3. *Economy.* By a single act of terrorism, the act serves to frighten tens of thousands, even millions, of people.

4. *Publicity.* Terrorists seek publicity, which in turn encourages terrorism. Well-publicized violence advertises the terrorist's cause.

5. *Individual therapy.* Fighting may be fun to some fanatics to a cause. Engaging in a battle gives purpose to life, and all the more to lives that are meaningless.

6. *Varied objectives.* One goal of a terrorist act is to exercise power and to get more of it. However, what power is used for may be variously conceived of by members of a group.

Those involved in ideological warfare against another group are willing to exercise violence in its most extreme form. The ideological framework contains the doctrines, opinions, and action plans for a group. The doctrine may include religious or political beliefs (Baron, 1993). In some groups there may be a combination of the two, resulting in a plan of action that launches violence against outsiders and in some cases violence directed toward their own members.

Why would the leader insist on mass murder of the group's own members? In this chapter we discuss two examples of ideological mass murders. The first is Jim Jones and Jonestown, the second, the more recent case of the Heaven's Gate cult. Jim Jones ordered the death of his faithful because he was certain that there was going to be some type of catastrophe initiated by the Soviet Union and aided by the inactivity of the U.S. government. Moreover, Jones told his followers that the U.S. government was a direct threat to the existence of his faithful. Jones said that this was proven by the visit of an American congressman. In the Heaven's Gate example, their leader ordered the deaths because it was their belief that there was a spaceship behind the Hale–Bopp comet, that had been sent to transport them to a better land. Their belief system was different from that of Jones, but the end product was the same.

Americans have been witness to several cases of political mass killings. We need to examine the mentality of this type of killer and demand to learn the manner in which such killers operate and possible ways to prevent such occurrences.

TRAITS OF THE IDEOLOGICAL MASS KILLER

The belief system of the ideological mass killer differs from those of other types of mass murderers. This ideology contains an element that is often political in nature and in some fashion is thought capable of changing society for the better. By murdering huge numbers of innocent victims, attention will be called to this position even if the position is not totally verbalized to the society at large. Certainly, the acts of the IRA in Ireland have resulted in the murder of untold

Case Study

Jonestown

Almost 1000 people were killed on November 18, 1978 in Jonestown. The Reverend Jim Jones ordered over 900 members of his religious cult to kill themselves. Most drank a poisoned mixed drink, some were shot, and others were stabbed. Jones suffered a fatal shot to his head. It was never determined if he shot himself or if he ordered someone else to kill him. The world was shocked by the enormity of the numbers and the tragedy that occurred in the forest of Guyana. What had happed there, and who was responsible for this catastrophe?

Jim Jones was born in Lynn, Indiana in 1931. As he grew into a young man, he became interested not only in religion but also in the suffering of the downtrodden. He was ordained a minister in Indianapolis. In 1963 he founded the People's Temple Full Gospel Church. He worked tirelessly for anyone who needed his help. He preached for racial and sexual equality. His group worked to find jobs for the unemployed and those who needed financial backing.

But there were strange happenings, too. Things were not all paradise in Indiana. Jones was known to have fainting spells and complained of poor health. He spoke of communicating with extraterrestrials, practiced faith healing, and often predicted the coming end of the world. Bad things were going to happen if "Father" (the name that Jones demanded of his followers) did not intervene. One major danger was the Soviet Union, which he was convinced was intent on bombing and destroying the United States.

Certain that since Indiana was in the midwest and would be a target of a nuclear holocaust, Jones was determined to lead his flock to safer ground. He fled to Brazil, where he lived a simple life. Some believe that at that time he was working as an agent for the Central Intelligence Agency, something that Jones never denied. There was no verification of this allegation. But to reinforce this perception, Jones often wore dark glasses that made some people believe him to be a special agent of the clandestine governmental agency.

After a short time in South America, Jones returned to the United States, soon after President John Kennedy was assassinated. Locating in San Francisco, he started his church again and became active in religion and fund raising.

From all outward appearances, Father Jones was a loving pastor. But not all was at it seemed. Some former members stated that he demanded absolute loyalty and obedience to his rules. For example, the members, once they became full members and the group had moved to Guyana in 1977, gave all their financial and worldly goods to the cult. They surrendered their identification cards, Social Security cards, insurance policies, bank cards, stocks, savings account balances, and so on. They truly lived in a communistic community.

Jones called himself Jesus and Lord, and it appeared that more and more, he considered himself to be a messiah. It was important that his followers also believed that he was the new messiah. To accomplish this task, Jones was successful in changing the minds of many of his followers to accept his doctrine. He did this through a constant indoctrination program that some said bordered on sophisticated brainwashing techniques. He convinced many that the end of the world was upon them. The United States was their enemy, but Jones had a plan for their survival and salvation. Only he and the members of his religious group would survive the holocaust that would come from the United States.

But there was trouble among the members and the families who were left behind. Messages were sent back and forth about conditions at the camp in Jonestown. In November 1978, congressman Leo Ryan and a small party arrived at the encampment to investigate the allegations. Talking with many members, most were complimentary of the manner in which they were treated and their relationship with Jones. However, two families wanted to leave with the congressman. As they boarded the plane to leave, they were ambushed and fired on by Temple gunmen. Five people, including Ryan, were killed.

Jones had told his followers prior to the shooting that Ryan and his party would be killed and this would bring the federal agents down on the group. They would all be killed. The only way to escape would be to commit suicide alongside "Father." Jones and his inner circle forced members to take the poison. Jones was apparently one of the last to die.

Can this entire unfortunate episode be termed an act of mass murder? It is our position that it can. Certainly, he did not take a cup to each person's mouth and force him or her to swallow the poisonous dose. But by his persona and charisma, he was just as responsible for the deaths of more than 900 innocents.

What could have been the motivation for the murder of so many victims? Is the motivation intrinsic or extrinsic? What is the anticipated gain? How are the victims selected? These and other questions are the foci of this chapter, which deals with ideological mass killers.

---

innocent victims. Their message of terror is directed toward society recognizing the injustices they have received at the hands of the British government. They have taken great pains to verbalize their ideology as well as their acts of violence. But there are others who kill masses of people whose exact motivations are unknown. The general typology of this killer is presented in Table 7.1.

Motivation: **The motivation is intrinsic to the personality of the killer.** With the ideological mass killer, it is readily apparent that the basic motivation for the mass killing rests within the personality of the leader. There is a search and a need for power and control. In this instance there is no greater power or show of control than to be the agent responsible for the deaths of a multitude of members of the group or cult. This is readily apparent in the case of Jim Jones and also of Marshall Applewhite of the Heaven's Gate religious cult. In both instances the message was that to obtain everlasting salvation, it was imperative to follow the directions of the leader. This was the only way not only to join God in the future life but also to remain in the good graces of the leader, who has somehow raised himself or herself to the position of a deity. Jones did this by calling himself Jesus; Applewhite, by being a prophet of God in a "container" on this earth. Heaven's Gate is discussed later in the chapter.

TABLE 7.1   Traits of the Ideological Mass Killer

Motivation
  Intrinsic
  Extrinsic
	The motivation is intrinsic to the personality of the killer.

Anticipated gain
  Expressive
  Instrumental
	There may be a mixture of gains for the killer; some material gain is recognized as well as a psychologically anticipated gain.

Victim selectivity
  Random
  Nonrandom
	The victims are members of the leader's group or cult. They are not selected randomly; usually, the entire group is murdered.

Victim relationship
  Affiliative
  Strangers
	The victims are not strangers to the leader of the cult; they are known members of the leader's group.

Spatial mobility
  Stable
  Transient
	The killer will move from one part of the country to another in search of new members or to escape notoriety.

Victim traits
  Specific
  Nonspecific
	Physical traits are not important to this type of mass killer; they are members of his cult or group.

Anticipated Gain: ***There is a mixture of gains, expressive and instrumental.*** The ideological mass killer, who kills typically by "proxy," hopes to achieve by the deaths of his followers a mixture of expressive and instrumental gain. In the first instance, if the leader does not die also, it is apparent that the death of his followers is a realization of psychological or expressive gain. The power and control that lead to the deaths of followers will convey a sense of ultimate control by the leader over the flock (Brault, 1993). In the second instance, the gain is instrumental or material. If the followers are no longer alive, their wealth and possessions are now the property of the group and ultimately the leader.

Victim Selectivity: ***The victims are not selected randomly.*** The victims at a mass murder scene are members of the leader's cult or group. In this instance, the victims are not selected randomly. They may not be known on an intimate basis as in the case of the family annihilator mass killer. This is especially true when the group is large, such as in the case of the Jonestown massacre. It would be less true in a case such as Heaven's Gate, where all 39 members of the group, including Applewhite, were killed. Each victim was known to the other if for no other reason than the relatively small size of the group. This type of mass killer does not select people to be fatally dispatched on a random basis. The victims are not selected from members outside the group. One reason may be that members of the cult do not interact with members of other cults in this fashion because it is only their group that they believe has the secrets.

Victim Relationship: **The victims are not strangers to the killer.** The victims of an ideological killer's mass murder scene are not strangers to the killer. In this instance, the victims are usually not strangers to the group's leader. Usually, although not strangers, they share no relationship, blood or marriage, to the killer. The relationship they do share is a relationship based on common or connected ideological beliefs. Again, witnessing the victims of the Jonestown and Heaven's Gate mass death scenes, the victims were not strangers and not relatives; they were members of the group who shared a common belief system that tied them all together. Of course, there may be some cases where a victim may be a relative of the killer—a spouse, sibling, and so on—but this is the exception rather than the rule.

Spatial Mobility: **The killer may move from one area to another.** The ideological mass killer tends not to be a geographically stable identity. There are some reasons for this, some obvious, some not so obvious. First, let us recall the case of Jim Jones. He started his People's Temple in Indianapolis, Indiana. Gaining some notoriety, he moved to South America and then to California. After a short period of time in the States, he moved to Guyana, where he finally settled into his own community, named after the leader himself—Jonestown. The movement from one location to another accomplishes several things. First, it is a way to attract new members who may not be aware of the group and its belief system. It was also a way to operate until someone becomes suspicious of the group's movements and activities. This was also true in the case of Heaven's Gate. Begun in Oregon, it moved several times until it finally settled a year before the believers left their earthly "containers" to join the spaceship that was in the shadow of Hale–Bopp.

Victim Traits: **Physical traits of the victims are unimportant to the killer.** Physical traits are not important to the ideological mass killer. The victims are all members of the cult and physical aspects are not essential to the victimization. The victims were both male and female and of all races (Jonestown's victims included whites and blacks; Heaven's Gate's victims were white, black, and Hispanic), and a variety of other physical traits were present.

Selected cases of cult murders are outlined in Table 7.2. To better understand the roles that motivation, anticipated gain, victimology, and spatial mobility play in ideological mass killing, let us examine the bizarre mass death scene of the Heaven's Gate cult (see page 81).

In effect, the suicide of the members of the Heaven's Gate cult was only slightly different from the Jonestown scene. It is not a scene of simple suicide. It is a case of a strong and trusted leader demanding the deaths of his followers. It is a case of mass murder, perhaps not strictly in the legal sense of the term but in the

Case Study

The Heaven's Gate Cult

In March1997, 39 people were found dead in a mansion outside the city of San Diego. The victims were members of a quasireligious cult named Heaven's Gate. Few outsiders had heard of this group before this act of mass suicide, but after, the names of the cult and its leader, Marshall Applewhite, became household words. Who was Applewhite, and why did 39 people take their own lives? These questions, and others, are not answered easily. The answers to their belief system is sketchy. We perhaps shake our heads when we think of the deaths of this small group of fanatical followers of their leader. What would compel them to take their own lives thinking that they would be taken up in a spaceship that was at that time behind a meteor? These are but a few of the concerns that came to the forefront immediately when the nation was alerted to the scene of mass death.

An informant told the police that he decided to call at the house since one of his employees told him that he and other members of the group were going to commit suicide. He said the members were going to leave their "containers" and catch the spaceship to go to heaven. After discovering the bodies, a call was placed to 911. Police and the media quickly arrived at the scene. The 39 people were reposing on their beds and cots, all dressed similarly and their shoes placed neatly by their bedside. Many had plastic bags over their faces and had died of poisoning and suffocation.

Where did this all begin? In the early 1970s, Applewhite started this small cult with the ideology that the end of the world was soon to come and the only manner in which to escape the catastrophe was to leave the earth once again. Applewhite preached a gospel that there was a large group of aliens who had come to earth from the 1960s to the 1990s to study the humans who populated this earth. The aliens were not male or female in the original form. They arrived on earth, "containers" were ready for them. The containers were of human form, some male and some female. Their mission was to study the earth forms and to report to those in the next world, the higher world, what earth was all about and how humans themselves behaved. The cult always remained small, probably no larger than 50. The members fervently believed the gospel of Applewhite and there were apparently few defections.

Applewhite was a charismatic leader, of the type sometimes called an "over-achiever." He was born in 1931, a son of a Presbyterian minister in Texas. He grew up moving from one location to another as his father started new churches. Talented in music, he sang in a few operas and taught music at the University of St. Thomas in Houston. He was also a choir director at St. Mark's Episcopal Church in Houston. Married with two children, he left his family in 1972 and met Bonnie Lu Nettles. They lived together in a sexless union until she died in 1985. Before her death they changed their names to Ti (Bonnie) and Do or Doe (Applewhite). Finally, in 1975, both claimed to be space aliens and convinced 20 people to leave their homes and move to Oregon, where they would meet with a spaceship. The spaceship never arrived. Undaunted, the group moved to California and resurfaced in 1993, when they took out an advertisement in a local newspaper proclaiming that the earth would be restructured. The members of his group were Christian-based angels sent to earth from the early 1960s to the present time. Finally, in 1997, the group rented a $1 million mansion in Rancho Santa Fe in California (J. Holliman, "Applewhite: From young overachiever to cult leader," CNN Interactive: *www.cnn.com/specials/1998/hgate.review/applewhite/*, 1997).

Applewhite apparently had the charm and charisma to carry out this plan. To illustrate the full impact of his leadership, it was reported that several of the men, including Applewhite, were castrated. This was verified by the medical examiner, Dr. Bryan Blackbourne (M. Kalfus and T. Saavedra, T. "Identities of cultists learned," OCregister.com/News & Features, *www.ocregister.com/1997/0397/cult/news29.html*, March 29, 1997). The medical examiner stated that all the bodies had a unisex look. Their heads were shaved and they were dressed in baggy clothes. This was perhaps the reason that it was first reported that all the victims were men. The physician also stated that the castrations were all "fairly recent" (CNN Interactive, March 28, 1997).

Why would a group of educated and intelligent people kill themselves at the insistence of their leader? What did they believe so strongly that they were willing to forfeit their lives for? What was supposed to occur after they departed from their "containers"? The basic belief was that the members of the group were killed so that the group could rendezvous with a UFO that was approaching earth. The UFO would be hidden from earth's view by the Hale–Bopp comet. As a friend of one of the "monks" of the group said:

> "All I can tell you is that they believed that they were going to be taken away by, as odd as this sounds, I'm just telling you what I heard, by a UFO."

> "That a UFO would come by and pick them up. Several months ago one of the members of the group who was one of the ones that committed suicide yesterday asked me if I was aware that there was a comet that would be coming close to earth."

> "They explained to me that they believed that there was a UFO following behind that comet and using it as a shield so it could not be detected by earth and that the UFO may very well be the one to take them away"

(Reuthers, December 24, 1997; *www.yahoo.com/headlines/special/san_deigo5.html*).

When the police arrived, they noted that there were no signs of struggle. The victims were lying on their backs, hands at their sides, with identical Nike sneakers on the floor next to the bed or cot. Their ages ranged from 20 to 72, and there were 21 women and 18 men. Passports and driver's licenses were tucked into pockets and a few of the members had $5 bills and quarters. The members apparently killed themselves in three groups: 15, 15, and 9. The first and second group were cared for by the third-group members (T. Saavedra, A. Mulkern, and M. Kalfus "Web of death," OCRegister.com/News & Features, *www.ocregister.com/news/1997/0397/cult/news.html*, March 28, 1997).

Applewhite had convinced the members of the group that the only way to escape the end of the earth was to transfer from their "containers" or bodies and join the spaceship. They would be transferred to heaven. The basic mission of the Heaven's Gate cult was offered by Doe in his statement:

What Our Purpose Is—The Simple "Bottom Line"

> Two thousand years ago, a crew of members of the Kingdom of Heaven who are responsible for nurturing "gardens'" determined that a percentage of the human "plants" of the present civilization of this garden (Earth) had developed enough

that some of those bodies might be ready to be used as "containers" for soul deposits. Upon instruction, a member of the Kingdom of Heaven left behind His body in that Next Level (similar to putting it in a closet like a suit of clothes) came to earth and moved into (or incarnated into) an adult human body (or "vehicle") that had been "prepped" for this particular task. The body that was chosen was called Jesus. The member of the Kingdom of Heaven who was instructed to incarnate into the body did so at His Father's (or Older Member's) instruction. He moved into (or took over) that body when it was 29 or 30 years old, at the time referred to as the baptism by John the Baptist (the incarnating event was depicted as "...the Holy Spirit descended upon Him in bodily form like a dove," Luke 3:22). [That body (named Jesus) was tagged in its formative period to be the receptacle of a Next Level Representative and even just that "tagging" gave that "vehicle" some unique sense of its purpose.] The sole task that was given to this member from the Kingdom of Heaven was to offer the way leading to membership into the Kingdom of Heaven to those who recognized Him for what He was and chose to follow Him. "The Kingdom of Heaven is at hand" meant that since I am here and I am from that Kingdom, if you leave everything of this world and follow me, I can take you into my Father's Kingdom. Only those individuals who have received a "deposit" containing a soul's beginning had the capacity to believe or recognize the Kingdom of Heaven's Representative. They could get to His Father only through total reliance upon Him. He later sent the students out with the good news that the Kingdom of Heaven is at hand, and His followers could help gather the "flock" so that the "Shepherd" might teach others what was required of them to enter His Father's House. His Father's Kingdom—the Kingdom of Heaven—in the literal or physical Heaven was certainly not among humans on earth. Leaving behind this earth included: family, sensuality, selfish desires, your human mind, and even your human body, if it be required of you—all mammalian ways, thinking and behavior. Since He had been through the metamorphic transition Himself from human to Level Above Human—under the guidance of His Father—He was qualified to take others through that same discipline and transition. Remember the One who was incarnated in Jesus was sent for one purpose only, to say, "If you want to go to Heaven, I can take your through that gate. It requires everything of you."

Our mission is exactly the same. I am in the same position to today's society as was the One that was in Jesus then. My being here now is actually a continuation of that last task as was promised to those who were students 2000 years ago. They are here again continuing in their own overcoming, while offering the same transition to others. Our only purpose is to offer the discipline and "grafting" required of this transition into membership in my Father's House. My Father, my Older Member, came with me this time for the first half of this task to assist in the task because of its present difficulty.

Looking to us, and desiring to become a part of my Father's Kingdom, can offer those with deposits that chance to connect with the Level Above Human, and begin that transition. Your separation from the world and reliance upon the Kingdom through its Representatives can open to you the opportunity to become a new creature, one of the Next Evolutionary Level rightfully belonging to the Kingdom of Heaven. (*Do's Intro: Purpose*)

From that message it is apparent that the followers were instructed that they were the new representatives and that the leader, Doe, was especially favored by the Father, who was his companion. The way to salvation was to return to heaven, the level above human. As most cults operate, the members were exposed to this constant message from Applewhite and were convinced they were the chosen people, the new representatives who were to go back to heaven in the spaceship behind the Hale–Bopp comet.

---

sense of the brainwashing and the message and mission proclaimed by Doe. It is a lack of understanding by professionals in the field of social and behavioral science that cases of mass deaths are treated as suicides rather than mass murder. Because of the message that becomes inculcated within the personalities of the victims, they see no alternative to following the message of the leader. The victims actually have little choice because to refuse to do what the leader demands they believe means everlasting damnation. In effect, Applewhite caused the death of his followers, and in this sense he is a mass killer in the same way that we believe Jim Jones was responsible for the deaths of more than 900 people in Jonestown. And the deaths attributed to the Heaven's Gate cult continue. In February 1998, Charles Humphrey, age 55, dressed himself like the other cult members found in the home. He was found in a tent with a tube rigged to a pump that filled the tent with carbon monoxide (*Courier-Journal*, February 21, 1998, p. A2). Will others follow? Possibly.

CONCLUSION

The ideological mass killer is different from other types of mass killers in several fundamental ways. First, the traits are different. We can see that by examining the traits listed in this chapter as well as in the chapters that treat other types of killers. In addition, the ideological mass killer often becomes a part of the victim count. The leader, the mass killer, will either kill himself (Applewhite) or perhaps have someone else do the killing (Jones). In either case, the killer dies with the other members of the group. Nonetheless, the leader is responsible for the deaths of the members of the group or cult. The leader makes the decision to preach the message that includes the deaths of the followers. Was David Koresh of the Branch Davidians different? Possibly not. The difference in the latter case would rest with the manner in which the members met their end. They placed themselves in a situation where the U.S. government through its law enforcement agencies was their instrument of death rather than the poison administered by the group members themselves.

Many Americans may believe that they are in no danger from the ideological mass killers, and this may be true. Although there may be little danger from this type of mass killer, the same thing cannot be said of many other types of mass

TABLE 7.2 Selected Cases of Mass Deaths in Cult-Related Incidences

March 1997	Three women and two men were found dead inside a home in Canada. They had been burned. They were members of the Solar Temple, a cult that believes that death will result in rebirth on a planet called Sirius.
March 1997	Heaven's Gate mass deaths occurred under the guidance of Marshall Applewhite.
December 1996	Sixteen members of the Solar Temple cult were found dead in a home in Grenoble. They had been burned.
October 1994	Forty-eight bodies of the Solar Temple cult were found burned to death in Switzerland. Six bodies were found in Canada burned to death.
April 1993	At least 70 members of David Koresh's cult were found in a compound in Texas. Koresh had preached a messianic gospel and called himself Jesus Christ.
October 1993	Fifty-three members of a cult in Viet Nam were found by officials. They had killed themselves thinking that they would go to heaven immediately after their deaths.
December 1991	Thirty people died from suffocation in Mexico after their minister told them to ignore the toxic fumes that were filling the church.
December 1990	Twelve people died in a religious ritual in Mexico. They died after drinking a toxic mixture of fruit punch mixed with industrial alcohol.
November 1978	The Jonestown mass deaths took place.

Source: This material was adapted from Cable News Network, Inc., 1997.

killers. What can be said with certainty is that this type of mass death scenario will not end with the Heaven's Gate episode. There will be other Jonestowns and Heaven's Gates. That is a certainty—a very sad certainty indeed.

Discussion Questions

1. How does the ideological mass killer justify the killing of innocent people?

2. What is the motivation to kill for most ideological mass killers? What effect do they feel will result from their murderous deeds?

3. How can the typology of political mass killers be applied to radical religious, political, and ideological leaders?

4. What role does the demonstration of power and control play for the ideological mass killer?

5. What does the ideological mass killer gain from the murder of either affected parties or innocents? Moreover, what is the relationship between this form of mass killer and his or her victims?

6. How does the ideological mass murderer maintain control over his or her followers? What key element in his or her personality often prevents dissension and keeps followers in a constant state of solidarity?

7. Why should the tragedies that occurred in Jonestown and under the leadership of Marshall Applewhite be considered cases of mass murder instead of mass suicide?

CHAPTER 8

The Set-and-Run Mass Killer

Early in 1955, a petty criminal by the name of Jack Graham was upset with his mother. She was a doting mother and tried to run the way that Jack lived. During the Christmas holidays, she visited her son in Denver. Upon her leaving to return to her home, Jack gave his mother a present to take on the airplane with her. The present contained 14 pounds of dynamite, and the bomb blew up shortly after takeoff. Forty-four people were killed aboard the aircraft. He was executed in 1957.

INTRODUCTION

Possibly the least understood type of mass murderer and the one most unlike the others is the set-and-run mass killer. There are several differences with this type of mass killer. First, this killer has usually left the mass killing scene by the time the police and other criminal justice professionals arrive. The killer is neither killed by the police nor commits suicide. There are other differences that are addressed in this chapter. This type of mass killer is most interesting and demands special attention from mass murder researchers and investigators.

What is so different about this type of mass killer? The victims are killed and the set-and-run killer is not present to witness his "handiwork." Certainly, these differences are subjects for study. There are also blendings of types in some of the killers. For instance, the Oklahoma City bomber, Timothy McVeigh, was a disgruntled citizen upset with the U. S. government. He was also a set-and-run killer, who set the bomb at the Murrah Federal Building. He was well on his way by the time the bomb exploded, resulting in the deaths of 168 innocent victims. What impels the set-and-run killer? That is the focus of this chapter.

TRAITS OF THE SET-AND-RUN MASS KILLER

The set-and-run mass killer has some traits that differ from those of other types of mass killers that we have discussed thus far. He has no inclination to commit suicide or to force the police to kill him. These and other traits separate this killer (see Table 8.1).

TABLE 8.1   Traits of the Set-and-Run Mass Killer

Motivation
  Intrinsic
  Extrinsic
	The motivation to kill is intrinsic to the personality of the killer.

Anticipated gain
  Expressive
  Instrumental
	There is typically an expressive gain for killer; in a few instances, the gain may be material.

Victim selectivity
  Random
  Nonrandom
	Victims of the killer are selected randomly; the killer is usually away from the scene by the time killing begins.

Victim relationship
  Affiliative
  Strangers
	Victims of killers are strangers.

Spatial mobility
  Stable
  Transient
	The killer tends to be a nomadic personality type and will travel from one location to another to initiate a mass killing scenario.

Victim traits
  Specific
  Nonspecific
	Physical traits are not important to the killer; victims are not selected according to traits or characteristics.

Motivation: ***The motivation is intrinsic to the personality of the killer.*** The motivation to kill for the set-and-run killer lies within the mind of the offender. The mass killer is impelled to kill because there is something within his personality that commands him to take the lives of innocent victims. This is evident in the case of Timothy McVeigh, Terry Nichols, and the unknown Tylenol killer. McVeigh was miles away from the Murrah Federal Building, as was Terry Nichols. The Tylenol killer, treated later in the chapter, was not on hand when the tampered medication was purchased or in the homes of the victims when the pills were ingested. With the Oklahoma City bombing case, the motivation was political. With the Tylenol case, the motivation is unknown but almost certainly there was a psychological motivation.

Anticipated Gain: ***The anticipated gain is expressive.*** For the set-and-run killer, the anticipated gain is certainly expressive or psychological. The motivation is intrinsic, so the traditional anticipated gain is also within the personality of the offender. In other words, this killer will not kill for financial gain.

   That said, there may be professional assassins who will firebomb for a political or cult cause and disappear from the crime scene before the killings occur. This is a subtype of the set-and-run mass killer. For this act of terrorism, the anticipated gain is financial. This type of killer better fits into the subcategory *mass murderer for hire*. In examining this set-and-run killer, it is apparent that he will kill for

Case Study

Timothy McVeigh

The case of the Oklahoma City bombing alerted the people of this country to the fact that domestic terrorism does indeed exist. On April 19, 1995, a 4000-pound fertilizer bomb exploded next to the Alfred P. Murrah Federal Building in downtown Oklahoma City. As time passed and more victims were found, this one incident of terrorism and mass murder became the largest act of mass murder ever committed in the United States. One hundred and sixty-eight innocent men, women, and children were killed in one explosion. Americans were stunned.

What kind of monster could have done such a thing? Initially, many thought it was the act of a foreign terrorist group. No American could be responsible for this act of mass murder. But they were wrong. An American citizen, Timothy McVeigh, an Army veteran, was responsible for the murder of so many people—a murderer who, when apprehended and convicted of the murders, would express no remorse for the murder of any of the victims, including the children. Who was Timothy McVeigh?

Timothy McVeigh was born in a small town in New York State. The town, Pendleton, had a population of about 5000 persons when he was born on April 23, 1968. In his childhood, there appeared to be nothing of great significance that drew attention to the crime that he would be convicted of later in his life. His parents, William and Mildred (Mickey), separated when Timothy was 10 years old, and they divorced in 1985. He stayed with his father after the divorce. The mother moved to Florida in 1989, where she remarried. She still resides in Florida.

McVeigh graduated from Starpoint Central High School in 1986. He was voted "most talkative" by other members of the senior class. There was nothing in his high school history that would indicate significant social or mental problems. But there may have been underlying emotional and mental problems that were not apparent to casual observers. For example, he did have an abiding interest in guns and weaponry, and he bought his first gun at age 13. He also read with great interest magazines concerned with guns and various types of ammunition. This is not to say that everyone who has such an interest will turn into a mass killer later in life. But perhaps he was suffering inner turmoil because of the marital problems of his parents and similar problems present in many young people. For whatever reason, he was a troubled young man. He was able to relieve himself of some of the tension by his interest in dangerous weapons. On a more positive side, McVeigh demonstrated some interest in computers in high school and had the computer nickname "Wanderer." It was later determined in court testimony how easy it is to obtain a "recipe" for making bombs over the Internet. His experience with the computer and the Internet made it easy for him to download such information.

Timothy worked part-time while in high school. He worked at the local Burger King and at a small country variety store. (This store had a department that sold weapons and ammunition.) After graduating from high school, McVeigh entered a local business college, quickly lost interest, and dropped out before the end of the first semester.

In 1988, McVeigh enlisted in the Army. In the military he was apparently well liked and no information was forthcoming about potential serious mental problems. After serving in Desert Storm, he left the service in 1991. After his experience in the military, seeing some of the world and the conditions that exist in other countries, McVeigh came home with a different point of view concerning U. S. politics and the manner in which this country relates to other countries throughout the world. Within his own country, McVeigh told many of his friends that he was troubled about the treatment that the Branch Davidians received at the hands of the federal government. He blamed the government for the deaths of members of this cult group.

Coming back into the United States after his experience in Desert Storm, McVeigh was a different person as to his perspective on the manner in which the U. S. government not only interacted with other countries but with their own citizens. His philosophies almost demanded some type of action against the government, especially after the FBI's involvement with the Branch Davidian attack near Waco, Texas, in 1995. The attack on the federal courthouse building in Oklahoma City took place on the second anniversary of the Branch Davidian debacle. After his return from Desert Storm, he moved in with some other men onto the farm of Terry Nichols's brother, James. He became close friends of the Nichols brothers. Apparently from this friendship, a plan was developed to commit an act of domestic terrorism. At this time, James is not an official suspect in the case.

Because of the pretrial publicity that occurred throughout the United States on television and the other forms of media, a change of venue was granted. The trial was moved to Denver. The judge was also removed because his office had been destroyed by the bomb, and the defense attorney persuaded the court that the judge could not be objective in this case because he, too, had been victimized. U.S. District Judge Richard Matsch was appointed.

The trial began in April 1997 and four months later McVeigh was found guilty of the murder of 168 persons and was sentenced to death on August 14, 1997.

What would impel someone to kill scores of people? Where does the motivation lie, and what is the anticipated gain? In examining this case, we see that the motivation is different than with Charles Whitman. Both had been members of the military. Whitman was convinced that he was mentally ill and wanted some help that he never received. He no doubt knew that he was going to be killed atop the tower at the University of Texas. He shared with McVeigh some of the same interests of a mass killer (e.g., an interest in guns and weaponry). However, Whitman was not consumed with anger toward the U.S. government whereas McVeigh was convinced that something had to be done against the government and thus attacked a federal building with many federal employees inside. The motivation was intrinsic to the personality of this mass killer. Whitman, for example, wanted people to study him and gain some insight into his mind (and brain). McVeigh, on the other hand, is still convinced that what he did was not wrong. He has not expressed any regret or sorrow over what he did. He has never apologized to the families of his victims for their suffering. According to the ideology of the killer, there are no innocents. But there *are* innocents. There is no doubt that innocents were in the federal building in Oklahoma City and that they numbered 168. A co-conspirator, Terry Nichols, was arrested and charged on May 10, 1995, later found guilty, and sentenced to life in prison.

---

different reasons. The major and distinguishing difference rests within the motivation—extrinsic to the personality—and the anticipated gain—instrumental or financial.

Victim Selectivity: ***The victims are selected randomly.*** The victims of this mass murder are selected randomly. The site, however, is selected for a reason. The victims just happen to be there. Consider again the case of Timothy McVeigh. In his mass murder, he never entered the Murrah Federal Building. He never viewed the 168 victims, never went to the day care center and saw the children he was about to kill. The building was bombed, and the two killers were not in the vicinity. Nichols was far removed, perhaps in Michigan, and McVeigh was driving away when fortunately, he was stopped by an alert police officer. There was no selection process. We remember how the disgruntled employee will return to his place of work and seek out those who have offended him. Joseph Wesbecker returned to his plant to seek out the supervisors, only to kill other fellow employees. Although the victims were not total strangers, they were not family members (the family annihilator). With this type of mass killer the victims are selected randomly with no concern for their relationship to the killer.

Victim Relationship: ***The victims are strangers to the killer.*** Victims of the set-and-run killer are strangers to the killer. The victims are not selected by physical traits or even the manner in which they are dressed or carry out their daily lives. They happen to be in the place the set-and-run killer has selected as the target for his actions, whatever the reasons may be. This was certainly true with McVeigh and the Oklahoma City bombing case. It is also true in the case of the Tylenol case. It is also true in the case of Julio Gonzalez.

Julio Gonzalez came to the United States in 1980 on the Cuban Mariel boat lift. He lived initially in Florida, then came to New York. Trying to settle into the American lifestyle, Julio developed a relationship with a young woman, Lydia Feliciano. Their apparently stormy relationship soon disintegrated. One night in 1990, they were at the Happy Land Social Club in the Bronx. Gonzalez saw his ex-girlfriend, Lydia Feliciano, dancing with another man, and he apparently became insanely jealous. He left the club and returned a short time later with a small container of gasoline. He set fire to the entrance of the social club and 87 people were murdered. There were only six survivors, one of whom was Ms. Feliciano.

In this case, 92 people in this club were strangers to Gonzalez. The only known victim was Lydia Feliciano. After setting the fire, he ran from the scene, only to be identified by people who were on the street at the time the fire was set.

Spatial Mobility: ***The killer tends to be nomadic.*** The set-and-run killer tends to be nomadic. This is evident in the cases cited. Nichols and McVeigh were not residents of the Oklahoma City area. In the case of the Tylenol killer, although the killer has not been apprehended, the profile suggests that he has moved from one location to another. Gonzalez relocated from Cuba to Florida and then to New York. It may be that this type of mass killer will move from one area to another to seek out "appropriate" places to carry out murderous acts.

Victim traits: ***Physical traits of the victims are unimportant to the killer.*** The physical traits of the victims of this killer are unimportant. Victims are selected

Case Study

The Tylenol Mass Killer

In 1982, seven people from different backgrounds and neighborhoods in and around Chicago, Illinois were murdered. They died from cyanide poisoning from altered Tylenol medication. These seven people, five females and two males, all fairly young, were the first to have died from altered medication available from over-the-counter medication (see Table 8.2).

Three of the victims were from the same family. Two of these victims were grief stricken at the sudden death of a member of their family and took the Tylenol to aid in their feelings of despair. One victim was a new mother. The 12-year-old had a bad cold.

The routes of the stores that sold the Tylenol products was a circular one along the highway routes 90/94, 290, and 294. It appears the mass killer stole the product some days or weeks beforehand, emptied the contents of the capsules and then replaced the capsules with 65 milligrams of cyanide, 90 percent pure, more than 10,000 times the amount needed to kill someone.

The motive for the tampering is unknown, since the killer has never been caught. Some believe that the killer was an employee of the company that manufactures Tylenol, Johnson & Johnson. Certainly the stock of the company dropped dramatically. It was not determined that any victims possessed a trait that would have made them targets for murder. For example, none was wealthy and there were no large insurance policies on any of the victims. The motive does not appear to involve any form of direct profit for the unknown killer. It has to do with another motive, intrinsic to the personality of the killer with an anticipated gain that is psychological rather than monetary. Perhaps a motivation was to show the American public that the government could not protect them from harm's way. These are some of the beliefs about the killer:

- The Tylenol killer is a white male.
- He was in his 20s at the time of the incident.
- He probably lived in the Chicago area.

TABLE 8.2   Victims of the Tylenol Killer

Name	*Age*	*Residence*
Adam Janus	27	Arlington Heights
Stanley Janus	25	Lisle
Theresa Janus	19	Arlington Heights
Mary Kellerman	12	Elk Grove Village
Mary McFarland	31	Elmhurst
Paula Prince	35	Chicago
Mary Reiner	27	Winfield

- He had some form of transportation (e.g., car or truck).
- He was clever but not intelligent.
- He was a shoplifter.
- He had few friends and no long-lasting relationship.
- He had a limited income and works in a low-paying job.
- He had a college degree but is underemployed.
- His objective was never realized.

Developing a psychological profile of the mass killer became a fascinating project for law enforcement and mass media. The components of the profile included the following:

- He had an Associate of Arts degree in liberal studies.
- He had trouble holding a job and cannot get along with people.
- He wore glasses.
- He probably used drugs.
- He played pranks on people.
- He probably had a morbid sense of humor.
- He probably moved from Chicago after the crimes.
- He still lives in the area around Chicago, probably with his parents.
- He has a collection of publications concerning drugs.
- In college he may have majored in photography or cinematography.
- He was a good liar.
- He had a violent temper.
- He was a domineering person.
- He had a minor criminal record.
- He may continue to do this crime using other products.
  (www.personal.psu.edu/users/w/x/wxk116/tylenol/)

The accuracy of the profile remains unknown. Will the mass killer ever be apprehended? Perhaps. However, the more time that passes, the fewer the chances of a successful resolution of this case.

---

only because they happen to be in a targeted area. Consider the victims of McVeigh and Nichols. Some were government workers, some were doing business with federal agencies, and some were children at the day care center. There were no similar traits or characteristics. This makes it all the more frightening. There may be no protection for us from this or any other mass killer.

There have been other similar crimes. In other areas, Excedrin, Lipton Cup-a-Soup, and Goody's Headache Powder have all been tampered with, although no deaths have occurred. In another incident, Tylenol was again tampered with, but thankfully, no one was killed. These types of incidents have diminished, partly due to the manner in which the products are now wrapped. However, tampering has not stopped completely. More than two score such crimes have occurred in the Chicago area.

CONCLUSION

The set-and-run killer poses unique problems to the serious researcher as well as to law enforcement professionals. Unlike other mass killers, who remain at the scene, either committing suicide or forcing the police to shoot them, this killer leaves the scene before the murder. This is certainly problematic and is a type of activity not confined only to the mass killer. One serial killer, the Unabomber, mailed packages that contained explosives that killed and injured many people. It took investigators two decades to make an arrest in this case. An arrest in the Tylenol killing case has not been made.

It is apparent that the traits and characteristics of the set-and-run killer are different from those of other types of mass killers. Because of these differences, the set-and-run mass killer poses unique difficulties. But one step is to acknowledge these differences and be aware of the activities and personalities of this type of mass killer.

Discussion Questions

1. What is unique about the modus operandi of the set-and-run mass killer that leads to misconceptions regarding his or her motives, intentions, and victim selection pattern?

2. Discuss the similarities of and differences between the mass killings by Charles Whitman and Timothy McVeigh. How were the motivations to kill and punish a large number of people similar, yet different?

3. What traits are possessed by set-and-run mass killers that are not possessed by any other type of mass murderer? How do you account for these differences?

4. For the set-and-run mass killer, what expressive gains are anticipated by committing the act of mass murder? What could the killer gain if he or she could never publicly take credit for the act?

5. How is the target, anticipated victim, or innocent victim determined by the set-and run mass killer? Of the three, which is more important to this type of killer?

6. What may the development and publication of a profile of the set-and-run type of mass murderer aid?

CHAPTER 9

The Disgruntled Citizen
Mass Killer

On December 7, 1993, Colin Ferguson killed six passengers on a subway in New York City. He wounded several others. His defense in court was that the United States was a racist society and he was a victim of that racism.

On June 22, 1997, Paul Crawford, age 74, fatally shot four members of the family who lived next door to him in Sauk Centre, Minnesota. Informants said that Crawford was angry because the children were playing on his dock at the lake and also that someone removed a stake from his yard where he had planned to build a fence.

INTRODUCTION

There is a group of people who are so angry and upset with the way the world has treated them that they lash out with mass homicide. Unlike, for example, the disgruntled employee, who returns to his former place of employment to kill, the disgruntled citizen is so angry and discontented that he or she lashes out at complete strangers with fatal violence.

The disgruntled citizen has traits and characteristics similar to the other types of mass killers. Like the family annihilator, this killer tends to be geographically stable. But as we examine in this chapter, the motivations and anticipated gains, victim selectivity, and traits are unique to the disgruntled citizen mass murderer.

In 1982, 21-year-old Hubert de la Tore was angry at his world. He had an argument with the manager of the Dorothy Am Apartments. To settle the score, he set fire to the building and 25 residents died in the blaze.

Such acts of mass murder are not solely an American phenomenon. For example, Thomas Hamilton, a scoutmaster from Scotland, was terminated from his volunteer position as scoutmaster because of his interest for young boys and his collection of photographs of young boys with bare chests. Two decades passed and he still had not been readmitted to the scouting program. He wrote to the Queen protesting his innocence and demanded some form of governmental action because his reputation had been damaged beyond repair. In 1996, Hamilton went to the Dunblane Primary School armed with four guns Like many other mass killers, he was a gun collector. He broke into a classroom and killed 16 children and their teacher. The children were 5 and 6 years old. Hamilton then turned a gun on himself.

In the United States, there have been numerous cases of mass murder by disgruntled citizens. We have already noted the case of Charles Whitman in Austin, Texas. Note that a distinction is made here between the disgruntled employee and the disgruntled citizen. The former returns to the unique source of his frustration, his workplace. The latter mass killer turns to public places to exact a senseless act of mass homicide: restaurants, schools, shopping malls, and other places of mass gatherings.

William Cruse, an elderly white male, decided to kill. He went to a shopping mall in Hollywood, Florida, and killed six innocent victims. Again in Florida, Carl Brown was apparently dissatisfied with the work of a local machine shop on his power mower. He rode to the machine shop and killed eight employees. He rode back toward his home on a bicycle was overtaken by witnesses who saw the crime. They shot him and then ran over him with their cars to ensure that he was dead.

In California, Gian Ferri had encountered financial ruin when his small business failed. Angry, he killed eight people and then turned his weapon on himself. An early mass killer of this type was Howard Unruh. In 1949, he killed 13 people in less than 15 minutes. Ronald Smith (a.k.a. Abudunde Mulocko), a black activist, was upset with a landlord who was threatening to evict the owner of a small business. He entered the business, forced seven people into a room, and set a fire. He shot himself in the head and the seven people in the small room burned to death. Colin Ferguson believed that whites were responsible for his dismal existence. He entered the subway in New York and started firing at passengers. Six died. Ferguson was arrested, and at his trial he defended himself. His defense included a proposition that he was a victim of a racist society.

Alan Winterbourne was upset that no one would hire him. He went to an unemployment office in Ventura, California and killed three state workers. He was shot to death by police in the parking lot. Robert Benjamin Smith entered a beauty college in Mesa, Arizona and killed five people. He confessed his crime to police. There are other stories, but the number is so large that it would be impractical to recite them all.

Table 9.1 contains the names of selected alleged and suspected disgruntled citizens. One killer, James Oliver Huberty, has been chosen to illustrate the case of the disgruntled citizen mass killer.

TRAITS OF THE DISGRUNTLED CITIZEN MASS KILLER

The disgruntled citizen mass murderer is examined in the same format as the other types of mass killers in this book. Although this type of mass murderer is alike in some traits, there are distinguishing differences. Table 9.2 illustrates the unique traits (or characteristics) of the mass killer.

TABLE 9.1   Alleged and Suspected Disgruntled Citizen Mass Killers, 1980–Present

Name	State	Victims
Humberto de la Torre	California	Burned 25 people in a building
George Hennard	Texas	Killed 23 people in a restaurant
James Oliver Huberty	California	Killed 21 people at McDonald's
James Pugh	Florida	Killed 10 people
Ronald Smith	New York	Burned 7 people in a department store
Carl Brown	Florida	Killed 8 people in a machine shop
Gian Ferri	California	Killed 8 people in an attorney's office
Colin Ferguson	New York	Killed 6 people in a subway
William Cruse	Florida	Killed 6 people in a shopping mall
Alvin King	Texas	Killed his wife and 5 people in a church
Girley Crum	Oregon	Killed 3 adults and 2 children
Michael Vernon	New York	Killed 5 people in a shopping mall
Geoff Ferguson	Connecticut	Killed 6 people
Bruman Alverez	Missouri	Killed his family and a house painter
Patrick Purdy	California	Killed 5 elementary school students
Alan Winterbourne	California	Killed 4 people at an employment office and a police officer
Barry Loukaitas	Washington	Killed 2 fellow students and a teacher

Motivation: ***The motivation is intrinsic to the personality of the killer.*** In considering the basic motivation of the disgruntled citizen mass killer, the motivation for the murders resides in the psyche of the killer. The killer perceives that society or a person has wronged him or her, and he or she must lash out with fatal violence at those people who are reminders of the society at large. The motivation comes not from an outside source that demands retribution or revenge; it comes from within the killer. True, there are perceived wrongs experienced by this killer that must be righted, but it is within his mind that the origins for murder emerge.

Anticipated Gain: ***The anticipated gain is psychological or expressive.*** The gain to be recognized for this mass killer is expressive. Similar to the motivation, there is a personal gain here. The killer murders a group of persons who have no real role in the dismal situation in which the killer finds himself or herself. However, this is not important to the killer. The gain is psychological to the point that the killer is demonstrating the wrongs of society. People will now pay attention to his or her plight even though the killer may realize that because of his or her actions he or she will no longer be alive to bask in the "reflected glory" over what he or she has done. The action will bring the person to the attention of the public and will

TABLE 9.2   Traits of the Disgruntled Citizen Mass Killer

Motivation
  Intrinsic
  Extrinsic
	The motivation to kill innocent victims lies within the personality of the killer.

Anticipated gain
  Expressive
  Instrumental
	There is no material gain for killer; the gain is psychological or expressive.

Victim selectivity
  Random
  Nonrandom
	The victims are selected at random; the victims are in the wrong place at the wrong time.

Victim relationship
  Affiliative
  Strangers
	The victims are usually strangers to the killer; unlike the disgruntled employee, those selected are usually total strangers.

Spatial mobility
  Stable
  Transient
	This killer tends to be geographically stable, although there are some exceptions (e.g., James Oliver Huberty).

Victim traits
  Specific
  Nonspecific
	Physical traits are not important to this killer; the victims are strangers with no common traits.

realize for him or her a brief moment of national attention for what the killer believes to be important. Money, insurance, or business interests (instrumental gains) are not the issue here. Creature-comfort realizations are not important to the disgruntled citizen mass killer. It may be that the killer's "15 minutes of fame" is what is vitally important to illustrate the murderer's problems or plight.

Victim Selectivity: ***The victims are selected at random.*** There is no personal relationship between the victims and the disgruntled citizen mass killer. Since this is true in most cases, it would follow that the victims are selected at random. This is clear in the case of James Oliver Huberty (see next page).

Victim Relationship: ***The victims are normally strangers to the killer.*** The victims of the disgruntled citizen mass killer are strangers. This was clear in the case of James Huberty, for example. The victims bear no culpability in their victimization and are not aware of the happenings that are about to occur. Riders on the subway in New York who shared the space with Colin Ferguson certainly had no knowledge of what was about to happen at this killer's hands. Ferguson did not know the victims, only that they were on the subway car that he was riding.

Like Ferguson, William Cruse went into a public facility, a shopping mall, and killed. In both these cases, there was no known relationship between the

Case Study

James Oliver Huberty

Huberty was born in northeastern Ohio. He married, had two children, and seemed to be living the American dream. He lived in his own home and had several rental properties that supplemented his income from the Babcox and Wilcox Company near his home. But the U.S. economy was in a downward spiral. The plant closed, and Huberty was faced with financial ruin. He had to sell his real estate properties, including his home. Finally, Huberty and his wife decided to leave Ohio and move to California to start a new life.

Settling in the community of San Ysidro outside San Diego, Huberty could not find employment that suited his expertise and training. From comments made by his wife and neighbors in both Ohio and California, it appeared that Huberty was bristling with anger and hostility directed not only at the government but also at the President of the United States, Jimmy Carter. He blamed the Congress and Carter for the economic disaster that forced him to sell many of his personal belongings as well as to leave his home and move to a strange part of the country.

Arriving in California, and in some respects due to the economy at the time, Huberty was unable to find what was in his mind suitable employment. He secured a job as a private security guard. He soon lost this position and was unemployed at the time of the mass killing. His wife would later tell of his depression over losing what was his financial standing in the small town in Ohio, the mortgage companies repossessing several homes, losing his job, and after moving to California, losing his job as a private security job. He would practice shooting at a wall in the basement of his home, no doubt using the wall as a reflection of those who had caused his failures.

On July 18 , 1984, Huberty, his wife, and their two daughters visited the San Diego Zoo. Coming home, they stopped at the McDonald's restaurant within viewing distance of their apartment in San Ysidro. Huberty ordered Chicken McNuggets, fries, and a Coke for lunch. After eating lunch the family walked home. Mrs. Huberty decided to take an afternoon nap and went to the bedroom. After only a few minutes, Huberty came into the room, reached down, and kissed his wife goodbye. He remarked to her that he was going out to "hunt humans." She would later say that he often made those kinds of remarks and that she was not overly concerned. He liked to shock her with those kinds of remarks, she said.

Huberty left the apartment, turned right, and walked to the McDonald's where only a short time before he had eaten with his family. He walked inside the restaurant, and in about 20 minutes he killed 21 people and wounded 19 others. Several of the victims were children; others were merely stopping there for a quick meal. None knew Huberty; they were complete strangers. After a short time, police were at the scene and a sharp-shooter fired a single shot from a building across the street. The shot was fatal and Huberty fell to the ground, dead.

What would impel someone to go inside a place where he would kill so many people? Hennard did the same thing in Texas. Phrases such as "Was it worth it?" echoed from the mouth of this mass killer. No such statements could be attributed to Huberty. He apparently killed in silence. The message was the same: anger, revenge, and violence directed to people who shared no culpability

McDonald's was sued by Huberty's wife, who claimed that McDonald's was somehow responsible for this massacre: Had it not been for the food additives placed in the Chicken McNuggets, Huberty would not have killed those 21 people. She was unsuccessful in her lawsuit.

Huberty settled in a part of the country where a certain type of social support system was missing. There were no family members, relatives, or friends who could aid him in his growing feelings of discomfort. He was alone. Why did he attack innocent victims at an "all-American" restaurant? Was it because this was a symbol of American life, a life that was becoming more barren to him as time passed? Was it because this was where people gathered, often families, and that they all appeared to be happy and contented, whereas he wasn't? We shall never find the one true reason. Regardless of the reason, 21 people are dead and 19 others suffered wounds at the hand of a mass killer who selected them as targets for his frustration and anger. Like many other mass killers, he is dead and cannot share with us any of the reasons for his fatal actions.

---

victims and the killer. George Hennard drove his truck through the window of a restaurant in Texas and killed more than a score of victims. The victims were strangers to the killer, a trait of the disgruntled citizen mass killer.

In short, the disgruntled citizen mass killer does not usually select a particular victim because of a personal confrontation that occurred between the two. They are strangers and unknown. This is validated by research done for this chapter, looking at various mass killers who fit the profile of the disgruntled citizen type of mass killer. Obviously, there are some exceptions, as there always are when one deals with human beings and their behavior. Take, for example, the case of Paul Crawford cited at the beginning of this chapter. He killed four members of a family who were his neighbors—but this is the exception to the rule.

Spatial Mobility: **The killer tends to be geographically stable.** This mass killer tends to be geographically stable. The killer does not move around from one part of the country to another in search for victims and opportunities to kill. The person is from a community and will carry out the killings in that area. This position is true for most mass killers of this ilk. However, there are exceptions, as is evident in the case of James Huberty, who moved from Ohio to California. However, he did not move to the west to seek out victims; he moved there to start a new life with his family, a new life that failed to materialize. In this instance, even though he moved across the nation, he would still be considered a geographically stable mass killer.

Victim Traits: **Physical traits of the victims are unimportant to the killer.** Physical traits are not important to this mass killer. In this instance, the victims are strangers and are usually not acquainted with the killer. The mass murderer will seek out a place where people gather. He does not seek out victims who will be at a certain location. This is a vital distinction.

With the traits of the disgruntled citizen in mind, let us now examine a case of a disgruntled mass killer, George Hennard.

Case Study

George Hennard

When George Hennard drove his pickup truck through a window of Luby's restaurant in Killeen, Texas, the country was shocked by his actions, which took the lives of 23 innocent people and wounded 22 others before the police arrived. Like many other mass killers, Hennard killed himself rather than be placed in custody. The entire incident lasted less than 15 minutes.

Hennard was described by some as hostile and intense. This proved to be an accurate evaluation of his personality, as the crime would later prove. In shooting his victims, he repeated a phrase to the people he shot: "Was it worth it?" Exactly what was meant by that statement could never be explained completely. The Associated Press reported that an acquaintance stated that Hennard was terribly upset over the situation that was developing over the appointment of Clarence Thomas to the U.S. Supreme Court. He became enraged over the testimony of Anita Hill. Hill claimed that Thomas harassed her sexually when she worked for him years earlier. Visibly upset, the informant stated that Hennard screamed, "You dumb bitch! You bastards opened the doors for all the women."

What compelled the killer in Texas to kill? The exact motivation is unknown. It is not extrinsic to the personality; it is definitely within the mind of the killer.

George "Jo Jo" Hennard was a young man with a history of drug and alcohol abuse. The people in his community knew of his violent temper and the way that he would suddenly, without apparent provocation, launch into a tirade. Words used by his acquaintances to describe him included *loner, rude, combative, impatient*, and perhaps the most accurate, *troubled*.

Friends of this mass killer knew that he had been more than a recreational user of drugs. He was discharged from the Merchant Marine because of possession of marijuana. He went from one low-paying job to the next and at the time of his death was living with his mother. His father, George Hennard of nearby Belton, Texas, had not seen his son for over a year. Dr. Hennard stated to the press that he simply wanted to put his son to rest and move on with the rest of his own life.

On a sunny Wednesday in Killeen, Texas, at 12:41 P.M., Hennard drove his blue pickup truck through the front window of Luby's cafeteria. The police chief of this small town, F. L. Giacommozi, said that Hennard seemed to hate women. He had just broken up with his girlfriend and had a history of domestic difficulties.

Hennard opened the door of his pickup truck and went from one person to another, firing his guns, a Glock 17 and a Ruger P-89. Police stated that during the shootings, as he went from one victim to the next, he would say, "Was it worth it?" As he shot, witnesses at the scene said that he was calm and went slowly from one victim to the next. In the meantime, several of the 100 customers at the cafeteria at the time of the incident escaped through open windows and emergency exits. By the time the shootings had stopped, Hennard had killed 21 innocent victims (Table 9.3). The police entered the restaurant and engaged in a shootout with the killer. They wounded him, but he ended his own life with a bullet to his head. Killeen is a small town in Texas located within a few miles of an Army base, Fort Hood. The town was just recovering from the news that 11 soldiers from that base had been killed in the Desert Storm conflict. This is not the only community that has been shocked by a lone gunman who has ended the life of a large number of people.

Hennard was crushed by his belief that women were the cause of the problems that he experienced and announced his displeasure at women when he called them "vipers" and asked of those he shot, "Was it worth it?" Huberty was apparently equally displeased, but his displeasure was directed toward American society.

CONCLUSION

In any society there will always be people who feel disenfranchised from others and from society. Because of this perceived alienation, many will resort to fatal violence to resolved problems that besiege them. Fortunately, most will not. The

TABLE 9.3   Victims of George Hennard

Name	Hometown	Age	Gender
Steven Dody	Killeen	43	Male
Glen Spivey	Killeen	55	Male
Olgica Taylor	Killeen	45	Female
Sylvia Mathide King	Killeen	30	Female
Ruth Pujoi	Killeen	Late 40s	Female
Nancy Stansbury	Killeen	Unknown	Female
Su-Zann Rashott	Killeen	36	Female
Thomas Simmons	Copperas Cove	33	Male
Al Gratia	Copperas Cove	71	Male
Ursula Gratia	Copperas Cove	67	Female
Debra Gray	Copperas Cove	33	Female
Michael Griffith	Copperas Cove	48	Male
Venice Henehan	Metz, Missouri	70	Female
Patricia Carney	Belton	57	Female
Clodine Humphrey	Marlin	63	Female
Zona Hunnicut Lynn	Marlin	64	Female
Connie Den Miller	Austin	Unknown	Female
Juanita Williams	Temple	64	Female
Jimmie Caruthers	Unknown	Unknown	Male
James Welch Male		Unknown	Unknown
Lula Welch Female		Unknown	Unknown
John Romero, Jr.	Unknown	Unknown	Male

victims are innocent persons; they share no relationships, no space other than the space they share with the killer.

What can be done with persons who are affected so negatively by the pressures that are prevalent in society, the same pressures that many others learn to handle adequately and socially? Early identification certainly can help address a problem before it becomes a full-blown fatal incident. Hennard, Huberty, de la Torre, and others were all known to have severe problems before their acts of mass murder. Huberty asked to be seen at a mental health clinic preceding the killings at McDonald's. Others of the disgruntled citizen mass killer type have often sought help only either to refuse the help or to be unaffected by the help when it has been accepted. Interdiction and human services can be offered to those who are dangerous to people in our land. Our first responsibility should be the protection of our citizens. This is most difficult to accomplish unless we can first identify those who are of the mindset to murder and to offer them some type of assistance.

Perhaps it can best be said that U.S. society will continue to be beset with these types of mass killers. At this time is the best solution is early identification of the types of personalities that may emerge later as mass killers and early intervention by mental health professionals and other experts in an attempt to resolve problems before they turn into mass murder incidents.

Discussion Questions

1. What is the major difference between the disgruntled employee and the disgruntled citizen when it comes to selecting their targets or victims? Does he or she typically have a personal relationship with the victims, or is it more important to their psyche that attention be paid to the problem they are rebelling against?

2. What does the disgruntled citizen mass killer gain by killing his or her victims? What statement is the killer making, and how is it generally received by the general public?

3. Compare the cases of George Hennard and James Huberty. What role did anger, revenge, and violence play in the events leading up to their final murderous episodes?

CHAPTER 10

The Psychotic Mass Killer

In Middlebury, Vermont, a gunman identified as Richard Stevens shot three people near a college campus in this small New England town on April 17, 1996. His body was found in an apartment close to the college campus. He had killed himself. Some believed that he had dabbled in the occult.

Ellen Church had a long history of mental problems. Finally, in 1959, she was in such a psychological state that she killed her children because she thought they were insane and heard voices that verified that verified that belief. She was determined to be guilty of their murders and was sentenced to prison for her crime.

INTRODUCTION

Among all the various types of mass killers, there is probably no more mysterious one than the psychotic type. This type of killer has a severe psychotic condition, including a severe break with reality, and may hear voices or have visions. This person is not simply neurotic, that is, he has a condition that impairs his interaction with society on a daily or near-daily basis. Additionally, the person is not psychopathic and does not have a character disorder as outlined in Cleckley's *The mask of sanity* (1982):

- Above-average intelligence
- Absence of delusions, hallucinations, or other signs of psychosis
- Chronic lying
- Inability to feel sorrow or remorse
- Inability to learn from experiences
- Ongoing trouble with the legal system
- Charming and personable
- Unreliable

Psychopathy or sociopathy appears early in life, and by the teenage years, the person has had many brushes with the law. Fighting, truancy, bedwetting (as a young person), cruelty to animals, sleepwalking, and fire-setting are all early signs of a person who may develop into a psychopath (Nettler, 179).

Of course, not all psychopaths are criminals. But since many wish to have their own needs and demands met with no regard for others, many are likely to run afoul of the law. It may simply be that their own psychological demands run against the rules of society, and are judged more important. They disregard the laws of society in order to have their own needs be met.

Psychoticism is different. A person with a psychosis is one who suffers from a break with reality. This person may hear voices or see visions. Holmes and Holmes (1998a) mention the visionary type of serial killer who murders because of the voices that command him do so.

With a mass murderer of the visionary type, thought disorders are the keymark of the psychotic individual. Netter (1982, p. 155) mentions three characteristics of the psychotic person:

1. Grossly distorted perception of reality

2. Moods, and swings of moods, that seem inappropriate to the circumstance

3. Marked inefficiency in getting along with others and caring for oneself

The psychotic killer appears to be very much in the minority of mass killers. Actually, it appears from the research that we have done for this book that most mass killers are of the family annihilator type. The psychotic mass killer captures the headlines, however, and this leads many people to believe that any mass killer is psychotic and cannot control his or her actions that result in the death of innocent victims. The truth of the matter is that the number of psychotic murderers is relatively low. Let us examine the psychotic mass killer in the same manner that we used in earlier chapters.

In 1980, in Reno, Nevada, Priscilla Ford claimed to have had a vision from Jesus. He told her that she should get into her car and drive downtown. There, the Lord commanded Priscilla, a 50-year-old at the time of the killings, to drive on the sidewalk and kill anyone who happened to be in her way. After she had killed seven people with her Lincoln and injured 21 more, Priscilla was arrested by the police. Her story of her direct conversation with Jesus did little to convince the judge and then the jury that she was suffering from a severe mental condition that would interfere with her ability to understand what she had done or to assist her attorney in her defense. In other words, the court determined that she was neither insane (a legal term) or incompetent. She was sentenced to death, and at the time of this writing, she is the only woman on death row in the state of Nevada.

William Cruse, a retired librarian living in Florida, believed that his neighbors were continually talking about him and telling others that he was homosexual. Hardly the friendly neighbor, Cruse would curse his neighbors and the children in his community. On April 23, 1987, Cruse went to the neighborhood shopping mall. A shopper, Cruse thought, stuck out his tongue at Cruse, and this launched him into his killing rampage. He killed six people, including two police officers, and wounded 10 others. After he was arrested, Cruse could not recall the episode. Despite being diagnosed as paranoid schizophrenic, Cruse was found guilty of six counts of murder and was sentenced to death. He is presently at Florida State Penitentiary in Starke, Florida.

What are the differences between this type of killer and the disciple mass murderer who kills because of a commandment of the leader of the group? The latter example, and we used the examples of Charles Manson and the David Koresh cult families as examples, will kill because of the voice and appearance of the living cult or group leader. In this case of the psychotic mass murderer, the person is psychotic and the voices arise from within the killer. This murderer is in very poor mental health. There are cases in which someone has "heard" the voice of the devil or Satan and followed that commandment. Usually, such people are not mass killers simply because they were in a position to fatally dispatch a large number of people. Witness the case of Ricky Kasso (St. Clair, 1991), a high school student who killed a young friend who owed him a small amount of money. Satanism was apparently a minor contributing factor. Kasso later committed suicide in his jail cell with a shirt that he used as a noose. The motivation to kill appeared to arise within the religious identification that Kasso linked with his behavior, including his dress and mannerisms.

TRAITS OF THE PSYCHOTIC MASS KILLER

With the psychotic mass killer, murdering commonly develops after a psychotic episode that convinces the killer that a spiritual apparition or ecclesiastical voice has commanded the person to kill. As with all the other killers we have examined thus far, victims of the psychotic killer have no personal physical traits that attract the killer to them. They are simply in the wrong place at the wrong time. Let us now examine the various traits of the psychotic mass killer (see Table 10.1).

Motivation: ***The motivation is intrinsic to the personality of the killer.*** By the very operational definition of the psychiatric and psychological term *psychotic*, the psychotic mass killer is out of touch, at least at the time of the killing, with social reality. This killer may hear voices or see visions, but the source of the visions or voices rests within the impaired personality of the killer.

There may be some misunderstanding concerning the basic source of the voices or visions. From the perspective of the killer, such as Priscilla Ford, it might appear that the voices and visions came from God, that is, from outside the psyche of the person, who is then impelled to kill. But this is not the case. The voices or visions that demand the murderous act come from inside the mind of the killer. Therefore, the commandment to kill is intrinsic to the personality and thus in the mind of the killer. It is the psyche of the killer that accounts for the decision to kill a group of people. The killer's personality may be molded by experiences in

TABLE 10.1   Traits of the Psychotic Mass Killer

Basic Motivation
    Intrinsic
    Extrinsic
	The motivation of the killer rests within the personality of the mass murderer.

Anticipated gain
    Expressive
    Instrumental
	The anticipated gain for the killer is expressive or psychological.

Victim selection
    Random
    Nonrandom
	Victims are selected on a random basis by the killer.

Victim relationship
    Affiliative
    Strangers
	The victims are strangers to the killer.

Geographical mobility
    Stable
    Transient
	The murderer tends to be geographically stable.

Victim traits
    Specific
    Nonspecific
	The traits of victims are nonspecific, and the physical traits of the victims are unimportant.

the person's past, a medical condition that bears some culpability, or a unique combination of social, psychological, and biological experiences and conditions that account for the murderous mind and then the murderous act.

Anticipated Gain: ***The anticipated gain is psychological.*** What does the psychotic hope to accomplish in the fatal dispatchment of a group of innocent victims who share no relationship? The anticipated gain is either expressive (or psychological) or instrumental. In the latter case, certain physical elements are realized. For example, if the anticipated gain were instrumental, the killer would hope for some form of wealth, money, or other material gain. This is not the case for the psychotic mass killer, whose anticipated gain is psychological or expressive.

The psychotic mass killer hopes to gain a measure of psychological gain. It may come in the form of appeasement for the voices or the visions that the killer has experienced. In any fashion, however, it does appear that the act does result in a form of psychological pleasure for the killer. Priscilla Ford certainly felt some form of psychological release from her act of mass murder. Perhaps the "beasts" that were deep inside her [as with the serial killers' fractured identity (Holmes, Tewksbury, and Holmes, 1999)] bear some responsibility for the act of mass predation. But this is all within the personality, as is the anticipated gain.

Victim Selection: ***The victims are selected on a random basis.*** It is readily apparent that the psychotic mass killer does not select his victims because of any type of fetish, partiality (Holmes, 1997), personal relationship, or any other factor. The victims are selected randomly; they happen to be in a space shared by the killer at the time of the murder.

Why would this be so? There are some theoretical reasons to believe that this assumption is true. Let us examine the FBI's work on organized and disorganized crime scenes as well as on organized nonsocial and disorganized asocial personality types (Douglas and Munn, 1992; Geberth, 1991; Holmes and Holmes, 1996; Howlett, Hanfland, and Ressler, 1986; Ressler, Burgess, and Douglas, 1988). The early groundbreaking work of the FBI's Behavioral Science Unit (BSU), led by Campbell, Douglas, Ressler, Hazelwood, DePue, and others, paved the way for an examination of the type of person who could commit certain types of crimes, especially violent and serial crimes. In their work they coined two terms that have been tremendous aids in the intellectual examination of personality types. The first type was the *disorganized asocial personality type*. This person had certain traits and characteristics that distinguished him or her from the organized nonsocial type.

The disorganized asocial type of personality has certain types of personality traits that manifest themselves in the crime scene. The FBI's assumption was that the crime scene reflected the personality of the killer himself or herself. The disorganized offender, for example, would be more likely to kill close to where the killer lived, was later-born in the family, was less educated, and was involved in menial work, if it all.

The *organized nonsocial offender* was on the other end of the continuum. This killer, for example, was usually first in the sibling order, was better educated than the disorganized asocial personality type, and was able to travel farther from the place of abduction and the body disposal site.

In the early part of the 1990s, the FBI and leaders in the BSU dropped the last part of the label and focused on crime scenes. The terms were now *organized* and *disorganized crime scenes* rather than *organized nonsocial* and *disorganized asocial personality* types. We are not certain why this was done, but we have a theory based on our own experience.

One author (R.M.H.) was declared an expert witness in a southern state in a murder case. The police department contacted R.M.H. to offer a professional opinion about particular behavior in this case. On the stand, the defense attorney objected to the testimony since R.M.H.'s terminal degree was not in psychology or medicine (with a specialty in psychiatry). The judge allowed the expert witness status because the testimony was predicated on crime scene assessment rather than psychological profiling. Is there a difference? In practical terms, no.

Perhaps because expert testimony was often not based in psychology or psychiatry, the agency felt more comfortable talking about crime scenes and implications of crime scenes rather than making statements and assumptions about the personalities of offenders without a basis in academic expertise. In any case, the FBI has greatly advanced their work in this area, and it is used not only by the FBI but also by others.

The point to be made here concerning the psychotic mass killer is that such a person's psychological state would not necessarily permit the killer to travel great distances to do what he or she believes needs to be done. The murder is done within the comfort zone of the killer (e.g., near the place of work or the domicile of the killer) (Holmes and Holmes, 1996, pp. 148–165). This would have an influence on the method of selection as well as the relationship between the killer and the victims. This killer will murder strangers in a random fashion.

Victim Relationship: ***The victims are strangers to the killer.*** As discussed above, the killer will select people who are strangers and those who live close to where the killer works or lives. This killer will not travel long distances to select victims for an extrinsic motivation (e.g., money, business interest, political or ideological motives). The killer's mental state will not permit him or her to go long distances in the search for victims. In terms of "stalking" behavior, the search is kept to a minimum because of the killer's mental limitations and the challenges that these limitations present. Despite the voices or visions, this killer still feels more comfortable in areas that are familiar and thus presents no immediate danger.

For all these reasons, it is apparent that the psychotic killer murders in a mass fashion those who share a space with the killer. This does not mean, however, that the killer and the victims know each other. Often, the media interview people who live close to the killer or to the murder scene, and they will recall that this killer acted "strangely" and could certainly believe that the person was capable of committing such a crime.

Spatial Mobility: ***The killer is geographically stable.*** The psychotic mass killer does not travel around the country to find employment, new housing, or search of victims. This killer feels more comfortable looking at potential mass murder scenes in a familiar area. In this respect, the killer is more apt to live and stay in the same area for long periods of time. The one reason that he or she may move from one location to another is because the family of orientation may move and the killer follows, since the killer often lives with the family. If the killer either lives with his family or lives alone, he or she will probably kill in the same or nearby area. This killer is simply not mentally or intellectually capable of moving from one location to another unless that other location is a site familiar to the killer. The voices may instruct the killer to seek out victims in other areas, an exception rather than the rule.

Victim traits: ***The traits of the victims are nonspecific.*** As with the other mass killers, the traits of the victims are not important to the psychotic mass killer. The choice of victims is made by voices or visions. There is no indication that this killer will make a deliberate effort to seek out victims who are of a certain race, gender, or any other type of physical or group identification.

Case Study

Ronald De Feo

Psychotic mass killers are not new in the United States. For example, in 1873, Alfred Parker committed a most heinous act of mass murder. Leading a group of gold miners and prospectors, this mass killer killed five members of his group. He then ate their body parts not for survival but for sexual enjoyment. He thus combined mass murder with cannibalism and paraphilia (Gantt, 1952). In 1959, Ellen Church murdered her three children. She had been seeing a mental health professional who had diagnosed her as a paranoid schizophrenic. She had been suffering from delusions and hallucinations (Newton, 1988).

One case that captured the attention of a great many Americans was the alleged Amityville demonic possession case that occurred in early 1974. Ronald De Feo, 23, came home on the evening of November 13, 1974, and found his mother, father, two brothers, and two sisters dead in their home.

Prior to this murder, there were strange occurrences in the home. During the trial, Ronald stated that his father was an abusive and strict parent. He said the father was a born-again Christian, and that this occurred after Ronald had tried to shoot his father while the father was physically abusing his wife, Ronald's mother. The gun jammed, and the father's life was spared. The father took this as a sign from God that he was a chosen one, and that a miracle had truly occurred. The father started his life over again, dedicating it to the Lord's work. This happened a year before the parents were killed.

A strange story arose from the testimony of De Feo. He said that the house was possessed by strange spirits. He offered testimony regarding parapsychological disturbances and said that the killings were done because of demonic and similar possessive states. De Feo confessed to the killings the next day. He testified that he was watching a program on television when a young woman appeared on the screen and instructed him to kill his family and place the bodies face down on their beds. He then put all the spent cartridges in a bag and threw them into a canal. The ballistics examination matched the gun that De Feo used. He was found guilty of six counts of murder and sentenced to many years in prison.

In some instances, family members are selected by the psychotic mass killer. This occurs usually only when the psychotic killer's victims are murdered in close proximity of the killer as well and the killer's lack of spatial mobility in light of limitations on the movements of the killer as a result of the person's disorganized mental state.

CONCLUSION

Acts of mass murder by the mentally ill can probably never be eliminated. There are many mentally ill people in this country. Despite massive attempts to alleviate the pain and suffering of those afflicted with mental illness, not enough has been done to eradicate the problems presented to society by those who are mentally challenged. Although most mentally ill people pose no great physical danger, there will always be in our midst mentally disturbed people who will commit acts so heinous that we can only react with horror and disdain. Unfortunately, many of these people will have sought help for their problems but the help was not enough to prevent their acts. We witnessed this in the James Oliver Huberty case in California. Huberty did not see visions or hear voices as far as we can ascertain, but he was mentally disturbed at the time of his killings. This same was true in the case of George Hennard in Texas. But there are others who are even more disturbed. For example, in February 1998, a young mother killed her child and then committed suicide. She had been diagnosed with severe emotional problems. A teacher, she had only recently been awarded her doctorate and from all outward signs was apparently in good health, mental and otherwise. The neighbors stated that she was friendly but aloof.

What can be done about this form of mass murder? Since most of the time such a killer has been known to be a person with mental limitations and handicaps, and also since many such people have been exposed to some form of therapy, better identification of persons who have the potential to mix their mental illness with violence may be the best plan of action. Confidentiality of records certainly would have to be considered, but there must be some way to identify these kinds of personalities before they act in ways such as those we have described in this chapter.

Discussion Questions

1. Among the various types of mass murderers, perhaps there is no more mysterious than the psychotic type. Why does the psychotic mass murderer pose such a threat to law enforcement officials and behavioral psychologists?

2. Why is it important to label a psychotic mass killer as such and not simply consider the person as insane and having at one point murdered numerous people during a psychotic episode? What does labeling and studying the psychotic mass killer allow us to do?

3. If a potential mass murderer is hearing voices demanding that he or she kill, from where does the motivation to kill emanate? Is it internal or external to the person?

4. What is the anticipated gain for the psychotic mass killer of carrying out a murderous act? Is it some appeasement from the voices, some form of psychological release, simply a hedonistic act from which the perpetrator derives pleasure, or a combination of all of these?

5. What role does the organization of the crime scene play in determining the psyche and type of person who committed a particular crime?

6. What elements of crime scenes do you believe the profilers and agents of the Behavioral Sciences Unit of the FBI rely on to determine the motivations and behaviors of violent persons?

7. Why do you believe that psychotic killers often do not travel far from their homes when committing mass murder?

CHAPTER 11

Youthful Killers: School Shootings

INTRODUCTION

Littleton, Colorado; Paducah, Kentucky; Pearl, Mississippi; Springfield, Oregon; and Jonesboro, Arkansas are a few communities that have experienced a school shooting that resulted in the deaths of students and teachers. Names such as Eric Harris, Dylan Klebold, Michael Carneal, Luke Woodham, Kip Kinkel, Andrew Golding, and Mitchell Johnson are synonymous with this type of homicide. They entered their schools and murdered fellow students and, in two cases, their teachers. What can be said about the Michael Carneals, the Luke Woodhams, the Eric Harrisses, and other young people who commit such acts? That question is the focus of this chapter.

School shootings by youthful killers have occurred numerous times in this country's history. Table 11.1 is a list of only the most recent school shootings. Some of these shootings resulted in mass murder. We made a decision to include in this chapter school shootings that involved mass murder as well as both those with fewer than three deaths and those in which no fatalities occurred. In three cases (Stamps, Arkansas; Richmond, Virginia; and Conyers, Georgia), there were no fatalities. In Bethel, Alaska, Evan Ramsey killed the school principal and a fellow student. In Fayetteville, Tennessee, one student was killed.

There are other cases of young people who have perhaps been influenced by the fame and attention paid to these celebrated cases. In Alberta, Canada, a 14-year-old youth shot two students, killing one, the first fatal school shooting in Canada in the last 20 years. In Texas, five teenage boys were arrested and charged with plotting an attack on students at their high school. The boys were thought to have been planning their attack for several months. Several students told the authorities that they planned to kill in a smilar way in which the tragedy at Littleton, Colorado, occurred.

Armed youth in our schools pose a real threat to the safety of students, faculty, administrators, and others. It is imperative to know more about the psychology of those who resort to crimes of this nature.

SCHOOL SHOOTERS: A WORKING PROFILE

In examining recent school shootings, certain consistent behavior emerges. It is from such common traits that a profile can be drawn. Not all school shooters,

TABLE 11.1   School Shootings, 1996–1999

Date	Location	Description
February 2, 1996	Moses Lake, Washington	Two students and 1 teacher were killed when Barry Loukaitis fired on his algebra class.
February 19, 1997	Bethel, Alaska	The principal and 1 student were killed by Evan Ramsey at his high school.
October 1, 1997	Pearl Mississippi	The person's mother and 2 students at a local high school were killed.
December 1, 1997	Heath, Kentucky	Michael Carneal killed 3 students and wounded 5 at his high school.
December 15, 1997	Stamps, Arkansas	Colt Todd shot 2 students in his school parking lot.
March 24, 1998	Jonesboro, Arkansas	Mitchell Johnson and Andrew Golden killed 4 students and 1 teacher at their middle school.
April 24, 1998	Edinboro, Pennsylvania	One teacher was killed and 2 students were wounded by a 14-year-old.
May 19, 1998	Fayetteville, Tennessee	One student was killed by a youth who killed the boyfriend of his former girlfriend.
May 21, 1998	Springfield, Oregon	Kip Kinkel killed 2 students and wounded 22 others at his high school.
June 15, 1998	Richmond, Virginia	A teacher and a counselor were wounded by a 14-year-old at his high school.
April 20, 1999	Littleton, Colorado	Twelve students and 1 teacher were killed by Eric Harris and Dylan Klebold at their high school. They then killed themselves
May 20, 1999	Conyers, Georgia	Six students were injured by a 15-year-old boy who said that he was depressed after breaking up with his girlfriend.

mass killers or not, fit this profile, but common traits identify the type of person and personality who may resort to violence of this type.

White Males.   Seldom are females involved in the actual commission of a school shooting. A youthful female may purchase the weapon for the killer or may be involved peripherally as a friend or a member of a clique.

School shootings also involve youth who are primarily white. School shooters generally enter a school building and shoot students at random. Sometimes the victims are known on a personal basis; other times by sight. Although one can debate the various reasons for this difference, let us leave with the realization that this type of homicide is done overwhelmingly by whites.

Age. The age of the shooter varies with the type of school involved: high school, middle/junior high school, or elementary school. In the cases listed in Table 11.2, Johnson, Golden, and Loukaitas, attacked their victims in middle or junior high schools. The older shooters kill older students simply because they themselves are older and further educationally advanced. It is a matter of age of the shooter in the school and the availability of victims. The middle school shooter kills younger victims simply because younger students attend middle school than high school.

Student. The school shooter is typically a student at the school where the murders occur. There are some exceptions. For example, a shooter entered an elementary school in his neighborhood in Stockton, California and killed several youngsters. He was 24 years old, and had attended the school as a youth.

There is no entry into the general community looking for strangers to murder as with some adult mass killers. Mass murderer George Hennard, for example, drove his pickup truck through a restaurant window and then killed unknown patrons. Another mass killer, Colin Wilson, opened fire in a subway, killing six strangers. There were no relationships between Hennard and Wilson and their victims; they were only sharing time and space. With the school shooter, however, there is usually a relationship, however tenuous. The shooter and the victims attend the same school. They often are acquainted, if not on a personal basis at least in the sense that they have crossed paths in the hallways, classrooms, the library, the cafeteria, or some other part of the school complex.

Rural or Suburban School Settings. Most killings in a school that involve multiple murdered victims are located in a suburban or rural community. For example, Heath High School in Kentucky is located in a small community in the western part of the state. In Jonesboro, Arkansas, the middle school is located near the border of Missouri and Tennessee, many miles from the state capital, Little Rock. Littleton, Colorado is a suburb of Denver. Springfield, Oregon is a small community close to Eugene, itself not a metropolis.

Conversely, shooting in an urban school is usually aimed at a personal enemy of the assailant. Certainly, shootings have occurred in inner city schools where a troubled student used killing to settle a personal score or for other reasons. But for our purposes here, the latter is an example of a shooting in a school, not of a school shooting. Drugs, personal vendettas, and similar factors play more of a role in shootings in a school. The anticipated gain and the motivation for killings in an urban school environment are different from those involved in the school shootings described in this chapter.

TABLE 11.2 Selected School Shooters

	Michael Carneal	Mitchell Johnson	Andrew Golden	Kipland Kinkel	Luke Woodham	Barry Loukaitas	Eric Harris	Dylan Klebold
Age	14	13	11	15	17	14	18	17
Gender	Male	Male	Male	Male	Male	Male	Male	Male
Race	White	White	White	White	White	White	White	White
Weapons	5 rifles, 1 handgun	13 handguns	13 handguns	Rifle	Baseball bat, rifle	Rifle, 2 handguns	30+ bombs, rifle, pistol, 2 shotguns	30+ bombs, 2 shotguns
Number of assaulted victims	8	15	15	29	10	4	48	48
Type of school attacked	High school	Middle school	Middle school	High school	High school	Junior high school	High school	High school
Number of victims murdered	3	5	5	4	3	3	13	13
State of occurrence	Kentucky	Arkansas	Arkansas	Oregon	Mississippi	Oregon	Colorado	Colorado

Middle Class Background. The school shooter typically lives with his family in a middle-class environment. Carneal's father is an attorney. Dylan Klebold lived with his parents in a $1million housing development. Eric Harris lived close by in a subdivision where the homes were more modestly priced. Klebold drove a BMW! Harris drove a Honda.

These are not youths from deprived backgrounds. There is no daily concern for survival. Their economic futures appeared bright and secure. College is an educational goal for such a family, and it is taken for granted that the shooter will attend college. Kinkel's sister was in college. Klebold's older brother attends the University of Colorado in nearby Boulder. The families have bought into the American dream, but the school shooter has abandoned that dream and has chosen to end educational striving, even to the point of self-destruction.

Disenfranchised Youth. Personal histories of school shooters are amazingly similar. For example, shooters are often disenfranchised from the student body. Students would later tell newscasters and police that the shooters were "weird," outcasts of the student body. At school, they were often teased and tormented. Luke Woodham stated that he was often victimized by the popular students in his high school for reasons unknown to him. Thus many of these students are considered to be strange or different by other students. The killers reinforce these differences by behaviors judged to be antisocial. For example, when bowling, members of the "Trench Coat Mafia" would salute a member who bowled a strike with "Seig Heil." This kind of behavior serves two purposes. First, it alienates other students and onlookers. Second, it serves to foster solidarity in the members of the outgroup.

Outgroup Membership. School shooters will often become involved with other disenfranchised young people. They may start their own group in rebellion to the groups that exist within the school. Luke Woodham cited his affiliation with others who were satanists or occultists. Harris and Klebold belonged to a group called the Trench Coat Mafia whose members had their own uniform: long black coats, black boots, and chains.

An outgroup has its own identity and interests. The group fulfills a psychological need for the youth. Unable to find or keep friends within the school community, they seek others who share their values, prejudices, and antisocial propensities. This appears to be an emerging scenario for school shooters.

Interest in the Internet and Computer Games. Shooters often tell law enforcement personnel that they spend long hours on the Internet playing computer games. Many of these video games have a message of intense violence—total destruction of others—through shooting, maiming, and killing. The two killers in Littleton were reported to have played such games in both boys' homes. Their competitiveness was apparent to those who witnessed their games and they were generally very competitive with each other.

Shooters may join chat rooms on the Internet and converse with those who have similar interests, becoming familiar with various Web sites that cater to their interests and psychological needs. At the time of the Littleton killings, at least 32 Web sites were devoted to hate messages. The police confiscated the killers' computers and retrieved valuable information from their hard drives. This same scenario was found in the case of Michael Carneal, and his computer was sent to the FBI for information retrieval. To date, no information has been made public about the contents of Carneal's hard drive.

Interest in Weaponry.   School shooters are often fascinated by exotic weapons and bombs. In the school shooting in Colorado, the young men allegedly placed bombs in the school cafeteria. There were weapons found in the home of one the young men, a shotgun with the barrel sawed off. In Jonesboro, Arkansas, the father of Andrew Golden took his son on hunting trips as a young child, and as a 5-year-old, he posed as a cowboy with a rifle taller than himself.

It is true that guns by themselves do not kill people. But many people kill people with guns. These killers have access to guns. One young killer stole a gun from his grandparent. Carneal stole his guns from a neighbor's locked garage. In the Littleton case, there is a suspicion that a friend of one of the killers, a female, purchased the gun for the murderer. They use their wits and their friends to acquire weaponry to accomplish their designated mission.

Regardless of where weapons and instructions concerning their operation or construction are obtained it is apparent that these youthful offenders have an interest in weaponry if for no other reason than to carry out their perceived mission to kill. They also learn how to fire the weapons, sometimes from their parents, sometimes from members of their outgroup, and sometimes on their own. Some have also learned how to construct bombs from instructions available over the Internet, as was suspected in the Oklahoma City bombing case of Timothy McVeigh and Terry Nichols.

Foretelling of Fatal Events.   Like other mass killers, school shooters will often tell others of their plans to kill. The killers in Colorado told fellow students that "something" was going to happen on Hitler's birthday. Michael Carneal brought five guns to school the day before his fatal shootings. Kip Kinkel told another student that he planned to plant a bomb under the bleachers and block the doorway so that students could not get out. He added that he would also go into the cafeteria and shoot people with his .22 rifle because he had more rounds for that weapon than he had for his 9mm pistol. The student paid little attention to the comments, thinking that Kinkel was just trying to sound important. In a journal, Kinkel wrote that he believed that he was evil and consumed with rage. This rage, certainly a motivating factor, lead him to kill repeatedly in his school. He later pled guilty to four counts of murder and 26 counts of attempted murder. He received a sentence of 25 years for the murders plus additional time for the attempted murders.

Many young shooters give forewarnings of actions but are often not taken seriously by those privy to these comments. Since such violent youths often say obscene things, other students may pay little or no attention to these new statements, thinking they will not come to pass. The statements are considered as but new nonsense uttered by a student whom the others are used to hear "spouting off."

Secrecy. The daily activities of shooters prior to the fateful day are often shrouded in secrecy. The killers may retreat to a personal space of aloneness. They spend huge amounts of time playing video games and planning their attacks. If the killer murders with an accomplice, they share their time with each other. Klebold and Harris spent days together making bombs that they apparently hoped would not only destroy the school building in Littleton but kill a multitude of victims.

Even though some may foretell their shooting, amazingly the killers are able to keep their activities and interests from others. Maybe it is because few give their statements any credence. The parents are surprised when they discover that their child was making weapons and bombs in their own homes. Secrecy aids the planning and implementation of their fatal venture.

Motivation. There are mixed motivations in the minds of school shooters. Some are directing a message of hate toward school or racial groups. Others are directing their hatred toward fellow students for perceived personal wrongs. For example, Carneal went to his school to kill those who (in his mind) had insulted or demeaned him. He had only recently broken up with his girlfriend; this could have been a precipitating factor in his decision to return to school and kill not only totally innocent people but his ex-girlfriend as well.

The motivation, then, rests within the killer's personality. There may be others within the group who are aware of the impending disaster, but the decision is made by the killer. The motivation not only serves as an impetus for action but also as a rationale. As also in the minds of terrorists, there are no truly innocent. All who are murdered deserve to die. By killing a few, millions will hear of his actions and recognize his name. Thus there is a certain "economy" involved in this form of mass killing. Would any of us know the names of these killers if not for the school shootings?

Abandonment of Former Friends. Because of the feelings experienced at the school—personal rejections, teasing, and so on—a school shooter will eventually abandon former friends. He will find acceptance, solace, encouragement, and comfort with the members of his outgroup. They share many of his feelings and accept him for himself since they share many of his attitudes and values.

Some shooters attach themselves to groups devoted to a hate message or, like Luke Woodham, affiliate themselves with groups involved in the occult or groups that are on the fringe of society's acceptance.

Case Study

Kipland Kinkel

Fifteen-year-old Kipland Kinkel did not appear to be a young man who would become a school shooter. He was an athlete, amateur guitar player, and from all outward appearances, the "all-American boy." But there was something deeper inside his psyche, a dark side that would emerge and cause great pain and suffering for many people. What were some of these acts that showed this dark side? Police officers in Springfield, Oregon said that he liked to put firecrackers down gopher holes and in cats' mouths. Not all young boys do this; Kinkel did and no one seemed to be too concerned. But something beneath the surface welled up and motivated him to kill. He mentioned to a friend that he would someday like to place a bomb under the bleachers at his high school and explode it during a pep rally. His friend just blew him off, perhaps thinking that he was just trying to play the "big man on campus." But this was no act. His girlfriend, Rachel Dawson, age 15, said that he was "always bragging about making pipe bombs" and having them explode at the school during crowded events (*Courier-Journal*, May 22, 1998, p. A1).

Kinkel fits the general profile of a school shooter. He is from a good family. His father was a retired teacher from the high school where the attack would occur. The mother was a teacher at a nearby high school. At the time of the shooting, his sister was a college student. He lived with his family, who enjoyed a good reputation in this northwestern state. The home was expensive; there was no day-to-day concerns over survival. The family was financially comfortable, and neighbors said they were warm and loving. But there was a side that Kinkel showed to others that did not reflect such a blissful existence. The cruelty to animals and the need to fabricate and exacerbate his accomplishments reflect a need to be a part of a group, to be accepted. Only the day before the shooting, he had been suspended from school and placed in the custody of his parents. The reason for his suspension? He brought a gun to school. He was allowed to return to school the next day. But nothing could have prepared the school for what happened on May 21, 1998.

On that day in late May, Kinkel killed his parents before he left for school. He entered the school a little before 8 A.M., went into the cafeteria, and pulled a rifle out from beneath his trench coat. He then opened fire. In the aftermath of the shooting, 2 students were dead of a total of 29 victims. Students fled the scene, some wounded. One young man, Jacob Ryker, 17, a member of the school's wrestling team, was also shot. He ran toward Kinkel, tackled him, and held him down until other students arrived to help. School administrators rushed to the scene. The police arrived and arrested Kinkel.

After legal battles, including a battle concerning his sanity as well as an attempt to keep him in the juvenile justice system, Kinkel pleaded guilty. This failed. He was tried as an adult and was given 25 years to life to be spent in an adult prison once he reaches 18. He is presently in a juvenile institution.

This case will not be the last case of killing in a school. Kinkel is a mass killer, killing his parents and 2 fellow students. But his earlier behavior should have called attention to his problem, a problem that resulted in four dead and more than a score of wounded.

CONCLUSION

School shootings have become a social problem in this country. Shootings occur with frequency but not regularity. With almost each shooting, there is another similar shooting, a copycat crime, that sometimes leads to another death or at least an act of senseless violence.

What is it about these youths who enter their schools and fatally injure those whom they know and even those who are personal friends? Seemingly, there is a layer of personal violence in the minds of many of our youth. Luke Woodham, Michael Carneal, and others are venting their rage in wanton acts of personal violence. Certainly, there are after-the-fact traits and characteristics, but we could pay closer attention to students who exhibit early warning signs, such as becoming more hostile in dealings with family or peers, destruction of school property, possession of firearms and other weapons, self-injurious behaviors, and a sense of rage. Despite the pressures and responsibilities that teachers and counselors already carry, they must become more aware of these early signs. Schools must create a safe environment for students, faculty, and staff. There are several strategies for this, including physical plant changes, reducing class size, reducing enrollment at megaschools, increasing security, and other strategies.

Change costs money. Change also has a psychological cost. And change is painful. But change we must if we are to protect ourselves from those who commit the heinous act of school shootings.

Discussion Questions

1. What are some of the dynamics involved in school shootings that make them different from other forms of mass killings?

2. In examining the traits of the school shooter, which do you believe are most accurate? Why?

3. Do you believe that music and/or the Internet play an integral role in the motivation for school shootings?

4. Pick one of the school shooters discussed in this chapter and make a presentation to class. What sources did you use? Discuss the main points in your presentation. Are they in contradiction to material presented in this chapter?

5. What role do social institutions play in identification and prevention of a school shooting? Should a school be legally liable for a shooting on school property? Why or why not?

CHAPTER 12

Problems in Mass Murder Investigation

INTRODUCTION

When a mass murder episode erupts, people in a community, and in some cases, the nation, suddenly become aware of their own exposed position as well as the vulnerability of those who suffered at the hands of the mass killer. There is a great deal to be done by those within the criminal justice system, including reporting the facts of the crime and informing the families of the victims. There is evidence to be collected, emergency medical care to be rendered, killer identification, killer apprehension, case preparation, prosecution, and so on.

Regardless of the tremendous amount of energy dedicated to the successful resolution of this crime, the surviving victims and the families involved often are able to contribute little to this investigation. A feeling of hopelessness soon envelops them. We talked with several injured victims of Joseph Wesbecker and a common theme permeated their statements. They said they were upset mainly because they (the victims and the families) were often on the sidelines with little involvement in the investigation. True, they were asked questions about the incident, but after that, it was months or years before they were able to tell their stories in court. Many were told few of the details of the investigation. They had times to think about their own vulnerability; how close they came to death. Several survivors questioned their own survival. "Why," some felt, "did I survive and others died? "

There are certainly some measures that can reduce the risk of being a victim of a murder (e.g., being aware of circumstances, not placing oneself in an area where victimization is a possibility, etc.). However, with a mass killer there is little that can be done to negate all risks completely. If we look back at the various types of mass killers we have described, we can see that many victims are unknown to the killer. The family annihilator is an exception. The reader will recall that all the members of a family were destroyed by Ronald Gene Simmons. The disgruntled employee may know some of his victims, but most are known only as fellow employees, not as personal acquaintances and certainly not as friends. Many disgruntled employees, who set out to murder, will, when they encounter friends at the workplace, inform them to leave so that they will not be injured or killed. This was true of Joseph Wesbecker in Louisville.

The mass killer will kill and leave a community in shock over the heinous acts committed against innocent people. But what can be done to change the course of events not only for the primary victims but for others as well? That question is the focus of this chapter.

COMMUNITY REACTIONS TO A MASS MURDER

When there is a mass murder, whatever its type, there are immediate community reactions. The reactions to mass murder are longer-lasting and permeate the consciousness of most people in the area. There is also some feeling that something can be done on an individual basis about being victimized by a mass killer. The same thing cannot be said about a serial murder incident. Let us examine what happens to a community when a mass murder occurs.

1. *The locale of the mass murder, often the entire nation, is alerted to the incident.* When a mass murder occurs, news spreads across the country almost instantly. When the Oklahoma City bombing occurred on April 19, at 9:02 A.M., it was only a matter of minutes until almost the entire country knew of the incident. After only 90 minutes, the suspect, Timothy McVeigh, was arrested after a routine traffic stop 60 miles away from the scene. The media reported the arrest and people quickly became aware of the person who was suspected to be at least partially responsible for killing 168 people.

The same can be said of another mass murderer. Patrick Henry Sherill, a former postal carrier, was a failure as an employee. He had received numerous complaints about his work habits and his failure to deliver the mail. He left his workstation in the Edmond, Oklahoma post office one morning at 7:00 A.M. He walked through the post office facility and shot indiscriminately at fellow postal workers. In 10 minutes the killing was over. By noon, broadcasts were heard across the nation. The shooting was a top story on the major TV newscasts that evening. The September 1, 1986 edition of *Time* carried a feature story, "'Crazy Pat's revenge"; *Newsweek* also featured the mass murder in its story, "10 minutes of madness" (September 1, 1986). Word spread about killings at yet another post office.

In the case of Carl Drega, in the printed media stories appeared in *USA Today* ("Killer inflicts nightmare on N.H. town," August 21, 1997, pp. A1, A2; and "He had this monster in him," August 21, 1997, p. A3), as an Associated Press release ("2 state troopers, judge, editor slain in rampage"), and in the Louisville, Kentucky, *Courier-Journal* (August 21, 1997, pp. A-4 and A-8) and "N.H. gunman who killed 4 kept explosives on property." In addition, the local newspaper, *The Colebrook News & Sentinel*, published a series of articles that highlighted the personal stories of four victims. (In writing the story of Drega, the present authors were impressed with the cooperation that this paper extended them in securing information about the town and the murders.) National media were also quickly in attendance in the small New Hampshire town.

Perhaps because of the "madness" involved in an act of multicide such as mass murder, and our society's appetite for violence, it becomes imperative not only to spread the news but also to become fascinated with the topic itself. It is the type of material that spreads and sells.

2. *The impact of the act of mass murder is immediate.* The crime of mass murder becomes a concern to a community. The remarks of the people are dismaying but also fascinating. What kind of person would do such a thing? One author (R.M.H.) remembers being on a plane from Louisville to Dallas when it was announced that a worker had gone into the Standard Gravure Printing Co. in Louisville and killed several people. The stewardess told everyone about the murders over the intercom. One passenger was a reporter for the local newspaper and immediately called his editor for more news. His editor told him some of the details and wanted him to return to Louisville as soon as he reached Dallas.

The word quickly spread throughout the cabin about what Joseph Wesbecker had done. It was on the TV newscast when we landed at the airport and I (R.M.H.) found that a childhood friend, Sharon LaFollette Needy, was Wesbecker's first victim. I recalled many of our conversations when we were teenagers and how impressed I was with her. I lamented her murder.

There was no time between hearing of the mass murder and the reactions to the circumstances of the deaths of the victims of Joseph Wesbecker. It seemed that everyone demanded to know more about this man who killed people he worked with on a daily basis for over a score of years. Why did he do it? What was it about his background that would impel him to commit such an act? Was he mentally ill? What types of weapons did he use? What were his motivations? Was he dead? Did he kill himself, or did the police kill him? What part of town did he live in? What about his family? Didn't they suspect him of being capable of doing such a thing? Those and other questions demanded immediate responses. Many answers were forthcoming. How many were accurate remained to be seen. It was apparent that many immediate answers were incorrect and far from the core of the truth.

3. *The effect of a mass murder is short-lived.* When a mass murder occurs, panic spreads very quickly. For a short period of time everyone has the murder on their mind, and some make personal plans that would ensure their personal invulnerability to any type of fatal predation. In some communities there is an increase in the number of personal weapons sold. Citizens take it upon themselves to protect themselves, possibly because they perceive there is no protection currently available that would make them impervious to the mass killer. In the same vein, alarm installation companies experience a brisk

increase in the sales of home alarm systems. When the Wesbecker case broke in Louisville, I asked a local dog trainer about his business. He stated that he had experienced an increase in the number of people who had enrolled in his obedience training classes. He was also aware of an increased number of people who purchased dogs for personal protection.

After a short time, though, people forget the crime and everyday life returns to that—everyday life. The sale of weapons returns to a more normal rate; home alarm system sales return to normal; obedience training classes and the sale of dogs for protection return to their previous levels. The panic that caused the reactions soon dissipates. There is no longer a perception of impending danger; the mass killer is no longer a danger to the community. There is no one perceived "out there" who would repeat such a crime in their community. The danger has passed; the threat of bodily harm is no longer a possibility. So life can now return to normal with only a minute possibility of another such attack.

4. *There is an envisioned end to mass killing.* In communities throughout the United States, many people have been victimized by a mass killer. Those communities may still feel the effects of a mass murder. In Louisville, for example, people are more apt to remember the case of three women who were murdered by Beoria Simmons, a convicted serial killer. Simmons, a social worker, seized the women off the streets in the early morning hours. Their bodies were found the next day. They had been raped, then shot. When Simmons was arrested, the community felt some peace, but people are still affected by the murders. It can be that we perceive that serial killers select those in our society who are most vulnerable—young women and children—the favorite victims of mass killers (Hickey, 1997; Holmes and Holmes, 1998a). They are the precious among us. It may also be that the serial killer problem appears to catch most media and societal attention. We share a fascination with serial killers. This fascination is kept alive by the mass media. The same thing cannot be said of mass killers. He or she is somehow viewed differently and in most instances share no common traits or characteristics that are thought to be desirable. The mass killer is mentally ill, strange, or just "weird." The community just wants to put the entire incident behind and move on to a society free of mass murder.

We have been told innumerable times that serial killers are free, roaming across the country. The numbers are estimated to be anywhere from 35 to over 200 such killers (Holmes and Holmes, 1998a). There is no such generalization concerning the mass killer. Perhaps because of this dearth of information about mass killers, the community allows itself to fall into a sense of security (in some cases a sense of false security), thinking that a mass killing would never occur in their small world. They are not so certain about the serial killer, wondering perhaps how soon it will be before the killer terrorizes their community.

SPECIAL PROBLEMS IN A MASS MURDER INVESTIGATION

It seems that few weeks pass when some jurisdiction is not involved in a mass murder investigation. Some are nationally known; others are known to only a few in a local jurisdiction. The Oklahoma City bombing attracted national attention. There was a national search for Timothy McVeigh's accomplices. The Federal Bureau of Investigation, the Bureau of Alcohol, Tobacco and Firearms, and other federal agencies were called in immediately and committed their resources to the arrest of others who may have been involved in this heinous mass murder case. After McVeigh and Terry Nichols were arrested, charged, convicted, and incarcerated, people breathed a little easier knowing that they had been apprehended.

There are other mass killers who attract relatively little attention. In the seminars that we do for police departments for the National Center for the Study of Unresolved Homicides, Inc., we come into contact with hundreds of investigators annually. Only recently at a seminar in Louisville, Kentucky, the class was composed of homicide detectives from many states. We spent two weeks analyzing cases along with other experts in the field: Arpad Vass, a forensic anthropologist; Neil Haskell, a forensic entomologist; Donald Rabon, an expert in interrogation and interviewing; David Rivers, sergeant in the Cold Case Squad of the Metro-Dade (Florida) Police Department; Henry Lee, internationally known criminalist from the Connecticut Police Laboratory, Tom Lange, retired homicide detective from the Los Angeles Police Department, and others. The presenters as well as the students were well aware of the unique problems presented by a mass murder case as opposed to a "smoking gun" or "dripping knife" homicide. Several problematic areas are present in a mass murder case that are not present in other homicides. In this section we deal with a selected few of those areas, although their order or presentation may not necessarily be indicative of their importance in any particular mass murder investigation.

Determining a Mass Murder Case

Say, for example, there has been a fire in a building that resulted in the deaths of a multitude of people. Early in the investigation it may be determined that the fire was accidental and the deaths were the results of bad wiring. However, if the arson squad determines that the fire had been set deliberately, it becomes a case of murder. By investigating the pattern of the flame, flammable liquids, the "Y" pattern of the blaze, and other factors, such a determination is fairly trustworthy and easy to ascertain.

When the Oklahoma City bombing case was first announced by the media, it was not immediately apparent who or what was responsible for the explosion. Was it terrorism, foreign or domestic? What it a natural gas leak that resulted in an explosion? Only after investigation was it determined that this was a case of terrorism and that a politically motivated mass killer(s) was involved. It was indeed a case of mass murder.

Protecting One's Turf

In the investigation of some mass murders, the ugly head of turf protection may rise up. If the case is a high-profile one, its successful resolution by a certain agency would be major coup for that agency. In witnessing the Oklahoma City bombing case, the Bureau of Alcohol, Tobacco and Firearms and the Federal Bureau of Investigation were both involved in the investigation. The Oklahoma City Police Department was involved initially, as well as the local fire department. The crime occurred on federal property. Careful negotiations would be necessary to clarify jurisdictions and responsibilities.

Information sharing is often political. This may become more important when the chief law enforcement officer is an elected official or when some other high-ranking public official who has some control over the police agency is close to reelection. If the case is not handled properly, or is unresolved, there may be a negative impact on the political career not only of the law enforcement officials but also of career politicians. This is also obviously true when a federal agency enters the scene and demands jurisdiction. Any negative interplay among local, state, and federal agencies becomes a threat to successful resolution of the case as well as to the manner in which it is presented to the public. The spokesperson for the case usually is from the department that has taken primary responsibility for the investigation.

Determining the Type of Mass Killer

Upon deciding if this is truly a mass murder case, certain determinations must be made regarding the scope and type of investigation. Who should be involved in the investigation, and what should their responsibilities be? Who should command such an expansive and expensive investigation? If this is a multidisciplinary investigation, what department should handle what responsibilities, and what should be the role and responsibilities of each officer within that department and role sharing with the other departments? Once these and other questions are answered, other issues and problems will become a part of the investigation.

One problem that may result is determination of the type of mass murder case that is currently under investigation. As shown in earlier chapters, certain types of mass predators vary in their methods of murder. The disgruntled employee mass killer will kill in a chaotic fashion and the crime scene and kill site are the same site. Moreover, the kill site is filled with physical evidence. The set-and-run mass murderer, on the other hand, is usually far removed from the scene when the deaths occur. The professionally trained and educated investigator should be alerted to the various types of mass killers, the manner in which they select their victims, and other such pertinent items.

Dedication of the Agency toward a Successful Resolution

Investigation of a mass murder case is expensive. The number of personnel involved increase with the dedication of the department; additionally, there are other expenses that will increase with the size of the task force: telephone and other communication expenses; personnel allotment; administrative and secretarial support; supplies; and other incidental expenses, including expert help in the investigation itself.

The number of people and level of expertise involved in the mass murder investigation certainly will affect the expenses involved in the investigation of a mass murder case. This was apparent in the Oklahoma City bombing case, where the cost was exacerbated in the trials of McVeigh and Nichols. There are some who might say that the government and taxpayers would have saved a great of money had the trials and other legal expenses not been involved. Had the mass killed been at the scene and died there, the cost to the government would have been greatly reduced.

Training and Education of Responding Police Personnel

The investigation of a mass murder case is different from that of the traditional murder case. The education of such an investigator must include all the natural elements of a traditional homicide investigation, but it must also include those factors that are unique to the mass murder investigation and the mass killer himself or herself.

Mass murder investigations could take some hints from homicide officers who investigate sex crimes that result in murder. Often, there are evident methods of operation and signatures (Holmes, 1997). With the firesetter, for example, who may be a set-and-run killer, he may start his fires in the same fashion. The alert arson investigator, for example, might be aware of the similarity. This same thing could be said of the mass killer who tampers with a food product. If it is done in the same way each time—this may be his signature.

Identification of the Victims

In certain cases of mass murder, the victims may be so severely disfigured that visual identification is not possible. In the case of a fire or a bombing, for example, bodies may be so disfigured that experts may have to be called in to aid in identification. A forensic odontologist or a forensic anthropologist are experts who might render valuable aid in the gruesome task. Dental records, bone reconstruction, and similar techniques may be the only key. In other cases, the bodies are easily identified.

THE MIND OF THE MASS MURDERER

To resolve the mass murder problem in this country certainly will not be an easy task. Mass killers have been with us for a long time, and there is no reason to believe that there is an easy or realistic solution to this grave social problem. There is no understanding concerning the etiology of the mass murderer. Clearly, from this perspective, there is a unique combination of sociogenic, biogenic, and psychogenic sources that account for the mind of the mass killer. As we examine the lives of killers such as Joseph Wesbecker, James Oliver Huberty, Richard Speck, Carl Drega, and many others, we can ascertain that there are many differences in their backgrounds. Some come from close and warm families, or at least this is what it appears from the outside, and some come from families that are mired in pathology. Certainly, in each killer's background there must be elements that contribute to the mindset of the mass killer.

With this said, there must be some understanding of mass killers and the manner in which they harm their helpless victims. Only by an understanding the mass killer can an investigation truly begin. Only when education and training are combined with a special emphasis on the investigation, and hopefully, apprehension of a mass killer, can the process come full circle. The investigator can fully appreciate the ramifications of a mass murder case that is different from other types of murder under investigation.

CONCLUSION

In this chapter we summarize some problems in the investigation of mass murder. The problems exist to some degree in most, if not all, law enforcement agencies. Departments, from large urban to small rural agencies, have problems that are present in many types of murder cases and are exacerbated by the enormous task presented by the acts of a mass killer.

Departments that investigate a mass murder case encounter problems that are not ordinarily present in many cases. Some of these problems have been discussed. Perhaps only a few will be present in any single mass murder investigation. However, if only a few are there, the investigation is hampered by the special and unique problems presented.

What is so very important is that the investigator become aware of the special mindset of the mass killer and how the crimes of the mass killer are different from other types of homicides. The mass killer is a person often seen as a murderer who kills for no apparent reason. There is at least one reason, and the investigator must learn what that reason is. This becomes a part of the nonphysical evidence that must be considered during the investigation.

So what is the future of mass murder in the United States? This is not an easy question to answer. Certainly, there will be no quick end to mass murder cases. There will be those who will kill in the name of God, or another Charles Manson. Regardless of the motivation, there will continue to be cases of mass killings.

What can society do to lessen the number of innocent victims who fall prey to the mass killer? The killings that are committed in the workplace can be lessened by an aggressive and thorough identification of those who are "troubled." Special programs, aggressive therapy, and so on, can and should be a part of industry's commitment to a safer work environment. Those who kill their families often have sought help through private and public social service agencies prior to the mass murder incident only to be met with rejection or delay. The same or similar comments could be made about other types of mass killers.

There must be a concentrated effort from various social, religious, and governmental sectors to address this grave social problem. Only then can a reduction in the number of innocent victims can be realized. Is this only a dream? Perhaps, but it is a dream that can be realized with the dedication of people and resources sincerely committed to solving the problem of mass murder in the United States.

Discussion Questions

1. Of the seven types of mass murderers discussed in this book, which type is one least likely to protect oneself from? Why?

2. What effect does a mass murder have on a community? How long does this last? Why do you believe that a mass murder appears to affect the residents of a community for a shorter period of time than that of an unsolved homicide or potential serial murder?

3. Why do you believe that the public and mass media appear to be more captivated by serial murderers than by mass murderers? What effect has this had on our knowledge base regarding the mass or spree murder?

4. How may the claims of jurisdiction by a variety of law enforcement and government agencies disjoint the initial investigation of high-profile cases where many people are either injured or killed?

5. Why is information-sharing essential to the successful investigation of any case where a person's life or property is taken or destroyed? What initial steps may be taken to ensure that information is shared among all pertinent parties to a homicide investigation?

6. Why is it important that local and federal officials classify crimes (such as mass murder) early? What implications does this classification have on what agencies will be involved and which agency maintains jurisdiction?

7. What type of training must a successful investigator of mass murder possess? Should he or she be a homicide or sex crimes investigator, an arson investigator, specialist in the behavioral or forensic sciences, a firearms expert, or a combination of all these and more?

References and Further Reading

Abrahamsen, D. 1944. *Crime and the human mind*. New York: Columbia University Press.

American Psychiatric Association. 1978. *Diagnostic and statistical manual of mental disorders*, 3rd ed., rev. Washington, DC: APA.

Anson, J. 1977. *The Amityville horror*. Upper Saddle River, NJ: Prentice Hall.

Barnard, G., Vera, H., Vera, M., and Newman, G. 1982. Til death do us part: A study of spouse murder. *Bulletin of the American Academy of Psychiatry and Law*, 10, pp. 271–280.

Baron, S. 1993. *Violence in the workplace: A prevention and management guide for business*. Ventura, CA: Pathfinder Publishing.

Bartol, C. 1991. *Criminal behavior: A psychosocial approach*. Upper Saddle River, NJ: Prentice Hall.

Bauman, E. 1991. *Step into my parlor*. New York: Bonus Books.

Benford, T., and Johnson, J. 1991. *Righteous carnage*. New York: Scribner.

Bennett, W., and Hess, K. 1994. *Criminal investigation*, 4th ed. Minneapolis, MN: West Publishing.

Bensimon, H. 1994. Violence in the workplace. *Training and Development*, January, pp. 27–32.

Blackburn, D. 1990. *Human harvest: The Sacramento murder story*. New York: Knightsbridge.

Brault, N. 1993. *Inside the cult*. New York: E.P. Dutton.

Browne, A. 1986. Assault and homicide: When battered women kill. *Advances in Applied Social Psychology*, 3, pp. 57–59.

Bruno, A. 1993. *The ice man: The true story of a cold blooded killer*. New York: Dell Publishing.

Bugliosi, V., and Gentry., V. 1976. *Helter skelter*. New York: W.W. Norton.

Bureau of Justice Statistics. 1996. *Sourcebook on Criminal Justice Statistics, 1996*. Washington, DC: U.S. Department of Justice.

Cahill, T. 1986. *Buried dreams: Inside the mind of a serial killer*. New York: Bantam Books.

Cahill, J. 1990. *Postal workers on the edge: A study of mail handler job stress*. Glassboro, NJ: Glassboro State College.

Caputi, P. 1989. Death goes to school. *Esquire*. December, pp. 137–155.

Carmody, D., and Williams, K. 1987. Wife assault and perceptions of sanctions. *Violence and Victims*, 2(1), pp. 32–56.

Cason, H. 1943. The psychopath and the psychopathic. *Journal of Criminal Psychopathology*, 4, pp. 522–527.

Cater, J. 1997. The social construction of the serial killer. *RCMP Gazette*, 59(2), pp. 2–21.

Cheney, M. 1977. *The Co-ed killer*. New York: Walker Publishing.

Chesney, M. 1997. *The female offender*. Thousand Oaks, CA: Sage Publications.

Cleckley, H. 1982. *The mask of sanity*. New York: Plume.

Conway, Z. 1989. Factors predicting verdicts in cases where battered women kill their husbands. *Law and Human Behavior*, 13, pp. 253–269.

Cox, B., et al. 1991. *Crimes of the 20th century: A chronology*. Linwood, IL: Publications International.

Daly, M., and Wilson, M. 1988. *Homicide*. New York: Aldine de Gruyter.

Davis, R., Lurigio, A., and Skogan, W. 1997. *Victims of crime*. Thousand Oaks, CA: Sage Publications.

Dehart, D. 1994. The serial murderer's motivation: An interdisciplinary review. *Omega*, 29(1), pp. 29–45.

Dettlinger, C., and Prugh, J. 1984. *The list*. Atlanta, GA: Philmay.

Deu, N., and Edelmann, R. 1997. The role of criminal fantasy and predatory and opportunistic sex offending. *Journal of Interpersonal Violence*, 12(1), pp. 18–29.

Dietz, P. 1986. Mass, serial, and sensational homicide. *Bulletin of the New England Medical Society*, 62, pp. 477–491.

Dietz, P., and Baker, S. 1987. Murder at work. *American Journal of Public Health*, 77(10), pp.1273–1274.

Douglas, J., and Munn, C. 1992. Violent crime scene analysis: Modus operandi, signature and staging. *FBI Law Enforcement Bulletin*, 61(2), pp. 1–10.

Douglas, J., and Olshaker, M. 1995. *Mindhunter: Inside the FBI's elite serial crime unit*. New York: Scribner.

Egger, S. 1997. *Serial murder: An elusive phenomenon*. New York: Praeger Publishers.

Emmons, N. 1986. *Manson: In his own words*. New York: Grove Press.

Endleman, B. 1993. *Jonestown and the Manson family*. New York: Psychology Press.

Fisher, R. 1991. *Violence in the workplace: Crisis intervention at the Royal Park Post Office: A case study*. Washington, DC: U.S. Postal Service.

Fox, J., and Levin, J. 1994. *Overkill: Mass murder and serial killing exposed*. New York: Plenum Press.

Gantt, P. 1952. *Case of Alfred Parker, the man eater*. Denver, CO: University of Denver Press.

Geberth, V. 1991. Lust murder: The psychodynamics of the killer and the psychosexual aspects of the crime. *Law and Order*, 39(6), pp. 70–75.

Gilbert, J. 1986. *Criminal investigation*. Columbus, OH: Charles E. Merrill.

Goetting, A. 1993. Patterns of homicide among children. In A. Wilson, ed., *Homicide: The victim/offender connection*. Cincinnati, OH: Anderson Publishing.

Hagaman, J., Wells, G., and Blau, T. 1987. Psychological profile of family homicide. *Police Chief*, 54, pp.19–22.

Hale, R. 1994. The role of humiliation and embarrassment in serial murder. *Psychology*, 31, pp. 17–23.

Harris, T. 1981. *Red dragon*. New York: G.P Putman's Sons.

Harris, T. 1989. *Silence of the lambs*. New York: St. Martin's Press.

Hearn, J. 1998. *The violences of men*. Thousand Oaks, CA: Sage Publications.

Heide, K. 1993. Adolescent parricide offenders: Synthesis, illustration and future directions. In A. Wilson, ed., *Homicide: The victim/offender connection*. Cincinnati, OH: Anderson Publishing.

Heide, K. 1998. *Young killers*. Thousand Oaks, CA: Sage Publications.

Hickey, E. 1997. *Serial killers and their victims*. Belmont, CA: Wadsworth Publishing.

Holmes, R. 1990a. Human hunters: A new type of serial killer. *Knightbeat*, 9(1), pp. 43–47.

Holmes, R. 1990b. *Sex crimes*. Newbury Park, CA: Sage Publications.

Holmes, R. 1997. Sequential predation: Elements of serial fatal victimization. *Journal of Sexual Addiction and Violence*, 4(1), pp. 33–42.

Holmes, R., and DeBurger, J. 1985. Profiles in terror: The serial murderer. *Federal Probation*, 46, pp. 29–34.

Holmes, R., and DeBurger, J. 1988. *Serial Murder*. Thousand Oaks, CA: Sage Publications.

Holmes, R., and Holmes, S. 1992. Understanding mass murder: A starting point. *Federal Probation*, 56, pp. 53–61.

Holmes, R., and Holmes, S. 1995. *Murder in America*. Thousand Oaks, CA: Sage Publications.

Holmes, R., and Holmes, S. 1996. *Profiling violent crimes: An investigative tool*, 2nd ed. Thousand Oaks, CA: Sage Publications.

Holmes, R., and Holmes, S. 1998a. *Serial murder*. Thousand Oaks, CA: Sage Publications.

Holmes, R., and Holmes, S. 1998b. *Contemporary perspectives on serial murder*. Thousand Oaks, CA: Sage Publications.

Holmes, S., Tewksbury, R. and Holmes, R. 1999. Fractured identity syndrome: A new theory of serial murder. Journal of Contemporary Criminal Justice. 15(3), pp. 262–272.

Home Box Office. 1984. *Murder: No apparent motive* (film). Stamford, CT: Vestron Video.

Home Box Office. 1992. *The ice man tapes* (film). Stamford, CT: Vestron Video.

Howlett, J., Hanfland, K., and Ressler, R. 1986. The violent criminal apprehension program. *FBI Law Enforcement Bulletin*, 55, pp. 14–18.

Jenkins, P. 1994. *Using murder: The social construction of serial murder*. New York: Aldine de Gruyter.

Kadaba, L. 1993. Violence increases in the workplace. *Philadelphia Enquirer*, December 1, p. F1.

Kantor, I. 1995. Using murder: The social construction of serial homicide. *Criminal Justice and Behavior*, 22, pp. 451–455.

Kaufer, S. 1992. Violence in the workplace can be prevented. In *Security Topics*, Vol. 3. Palm Springs, CA: Inter/Action Associates.

Kelleher, M. 1997. *Profiling the lethal employee*. Westport, CT: Praeger Publishers.

Kenney, B. 1995. Serial murder: A more accurate and inclusive definition. *International Journal of Offender Therapy and Comparative Criminology*, 39, pp. 298–306.

Kushner, H. 1997. *The future of terrorism: Violence in the new millennium*. Thousand Oaks, CA: Sage Publications.

Lavergne, G. 1997. *Sniper in the tower*. El Paso, TX: University of North Texas Press.

Leitenberg, H., and Henning, H. 1995. Sexual fantasy. *Psychological Bulletin*, 117(3), pp. 469–496.

Lester, D. 1995. *Serial killers: The insatiable passion*. Philadelphia: Charles Press.

Levin, J., and Fox, J. 1985. *Mass murder: America's growing menace*. New York: Plenum Publishing.

Leyton, E. 1986. *Compulsive killers*. New York: New York University Press.

Losey, J. 1994. Managing in a era of workplace violence. *Managing Office Technology*, February, pp. 27–28.

Lunde, D. 1976. *Murder and madness*. New York: W.W. Norton.

MacCullock, M., et al. 1983. Sadistic fantasy, sadistic behavior, and offending. *British Journal of Psychiatry*, 143, pp. 20–29.

Madigan, T. 1993. *See no evil*. Forth Worth, TX: Summit Group.

Maguire, K., and Pastore, A. 1996. *Sourcebook on criminal justice statistics, 1995*. Washington, DC: U.S. Government Printing Offic.

McGinnis, J. 1985. *Fatal vision*. New York: Simon & Schuster.

Michaud, S., and Aynesworth, H. 1983. *The only living witness*. New York: Simon & Schuster.

Monahan, J. 1994. The causes of violence. *FBI Law Enforcement Bulletin*, January, pp. 11–15.

Nelson, C., Corzine, J., and Huff-Corzine, L. 1994. The violent west reexamined: A research note on regional homicide rates. *Criminology*, 32(1), pp. 149–161.

Netter, G. 1982. Explaining murder. Cincinnati: Anderson Publishing.

Newsweek. 1989. Death on the playground. January 30, p. 30.

Newton, M. 1988. *Mass murder: An annotated bibliography*. New York: Garland Publishing.

New York Times. 1993. Postal study aims to spot violence-prone workers. July 2, p. A19.

Nisbett, R. 1993. Violence and U.S. regional culture. *American Psychologist*. 48, pp. 441–449.

Norris, J., and Birnes, W. 1988. *Serial killers: The growing menace*. New York: Dolphin Books.

O'Boyle, T. 1992. Disgruntled workers intent on revenge increasingly harm colleagues and bosses. *Wall Street Journal*, pp. B1, B10.

O'Brien, D. 1985. *Two of a kind: The hillside stranglers*. New York: Signet Books.

Ogle, R., Maier-Katin, D., and Bernard, T. 1995. A theory of homicidal behavior among women. *Criminology*, 33(2), pp. 173–193.

O'Reilly-Fleming, T., ed. 1996. *Serial and mass murder: Theory, research and policy*. Toronto, Ontario, Canada: Canadian Scholar's Press.

Pallone, N., and Hennessy, J. 1992. *Criminal behavior: A psychological analysis*. New Brunswick, NJ: Transaction Publishers.

Peck, M. 1983. *People of the lie*. New York: Simon & Schuster.

Pollock. P. 1996. A case of spree serial murder with suggested diagnostic opinions. *International Journal of Offender Therapy and Comparative Criminology*, 39, pp. 258–268.

Potter, J., and Bost, F. 1997. *Fatal justice*. New York: W.W. Norton.

Prentky, A., et al. 1989. The presumptive role of fantasy in serial sexual homicide. *American Journal of Psychiatry*, 146(7), pp. 887–899.

Reavis, D. 1995. *Ashes of Waco*. New York: Simon & Schuster.

Ressler, R., Burgess, A., and Douglas, J. 1988. *Sexual homicide: Patterns, motives, and procedures for investigations*. Lexington, MA: Lexington Books.

Riddle, L. 1997. *Ashes to ashes*. New York: Pinnacle Books.

Roth, J. 1994, *Understanding and preventing violence*. NIJ Research in Brief. Washington, DC: U.S. Department of Justice.

Rush, G. 1997. *The dictionary of criminal justice*, 5th ed. Guilford, CT: Dushkin/McGraw-Hill.

Ryzuk, M. 1990. *Thou shalt not kill*. New York: Warner Books.

Sanders, E. 1971. *The family*. New York: E.P. Dutton

Sears, D. 1991. *To kill again*. Wilmington, DE: Scholarly Resources.

Seger, K. 1993. Violence in the workplace: An assessment of the problem bases on responses from 32 large corporations. *Security Journal*, 4(3), pp. 39–149.

Selzer, M. 1995. Serial killers (II): The pathological public sphere. *Critical Inquiry*, 22, pp. 122–149.

Sharkey, J. 1990. *Death sentence: The inside story of the John List murders*. New York: Signet Books.

Smith, C., and Guillen, T. 1990. *The search for the Green River killer*. New York: Onyx.

Smith, D., and Zahn, D. 1998a. *Homicide: A sourcebook of social research*. Thousand Oaks, CA: Sage Publications.

Smith, D., and Zahn, D. 1998b. *Studying and preventing homicide*. Thousand Oaks, CA: Sage Publications.

Spungen, D. 1997. *Homicide:The hidden victims*. Thousand Oaks, CA: Sage Publications.

Stack, A. 1983. *The lust killer*. New York: Signet Books.

St. Clair, R. 1991. Say you love satan. New York: Pocket Books.

Strickney, B. 1996. *All-American monster*, Amherst, NY: Prometheus Books.

Sullivan, G., and Aronson, H. 1978. *High hopes: The Amityville murders*. New York: McCann and Geoghegan.

Sykes, G., and Matza, D. 1957. Techniques of neutralization: A theory of delinquency. *American Sociological Review*, 22 (December), pp. 664–670.

Terry, M. 1987. *The ultimate terror*. New York: Doubleday.

Vito, G., and Holmes, R. 1993. *Criminology: Theory, Research and Policy*. Belmont, CA: Wadsworth Publishing.

Yochelson, S., and Samenow, S. 1976. *The criminal personality*. Northvale, NJ: Jason Aronson.

Index